Cottage Gardens

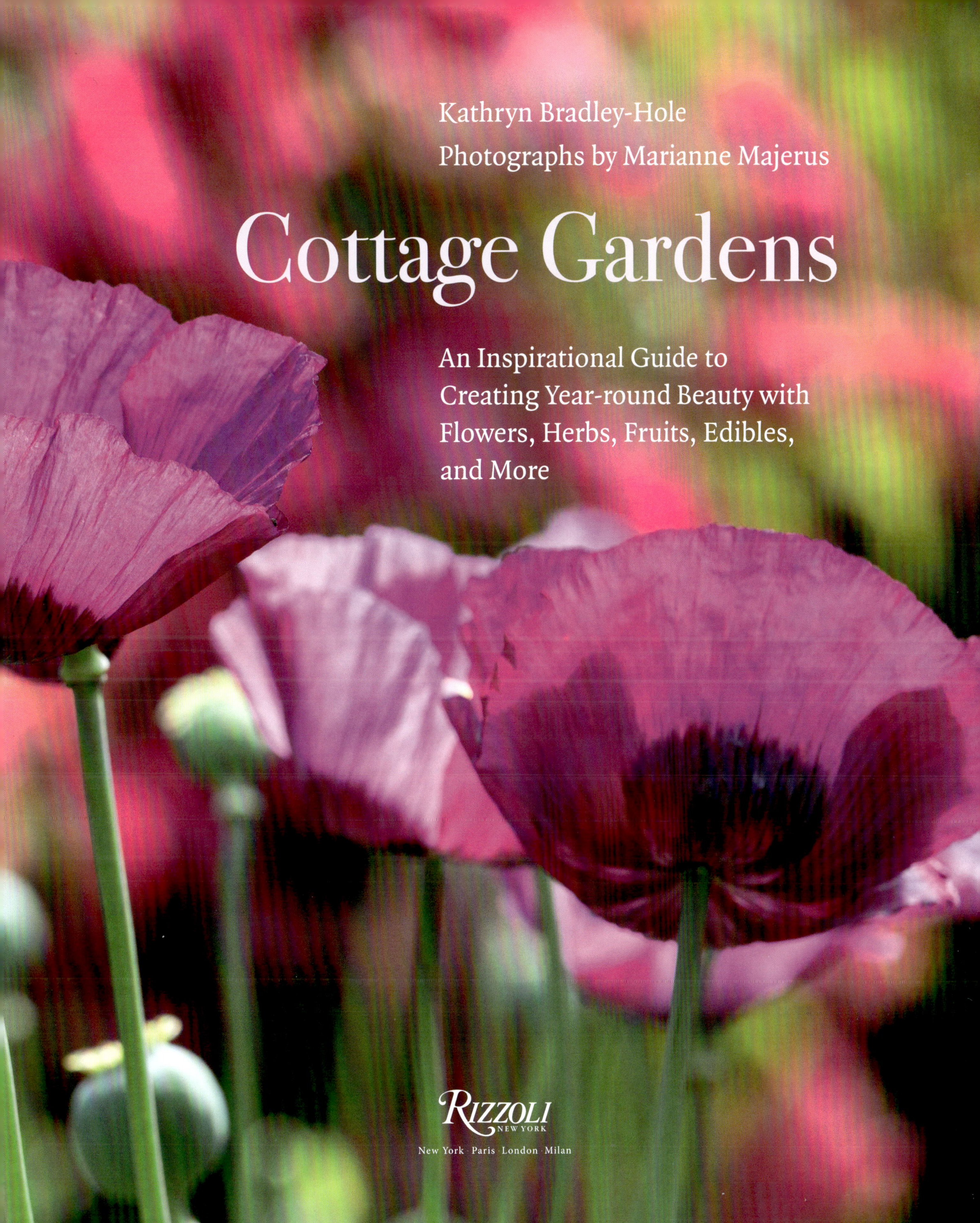

Kathryn Bradley-Hole
Photographs by Marianne Majerus

Cottage Gardens

An Inspirational Guide to Creating Year-round Beauty with Flowers, Herbs, Fruits, Edibles, and More

RIZZOLI
NEW YORK
New York · Paris · London · Milan

Contents

An Introduction to Cottage Gardens

THE SKY IS BLUE, WITH FLUFFY CLOUDS LAZILY DRIFTING BY. A straight garden path is brightened and warmed by sunshine, except where dozens of gigantic sunflowers cast flickering shadows across it. Bulbous pots, glazed in lapis blue and white, are packed with scarlet and pink gladioli, their rigid wands erupting like fireworks at regular intervals along the path, where a small child stands beside the floral abundance. Two more small figures are descending a rustic garden stairway, which itself is garlanded with a tangle of deep red nasturtiums. In *The Artist's Garden at Vétheuil*, 1881, Claude Monet distilled the carefree essence of cottage garden style. The scene is a relaxed milieu, having been created centuries earlier for very practical reasons; but in the nineteenth century, the cottage and its unregimented, seasonal garden gained momentum as a pleasing and enormously popular topic for artists and writers, both amateur and professional.

There are various reasons for this, and we shall encounter, in the course of this book, some of the cast of characters who brought cottage garden style to the fore during Monet's lifetime and after, since the appeal of a cottage garden is timeless. It is also a familiar aesthetic that has been exported around the world and continues to be appreciated for its apparently carefree abundance and charm.

Although the style often appears quite unstructured and without hierarchy or symmetry, it has long been adopted very successfully in gardens of almost any size and is frequently attached to houses far too grand to be regarded as cottages. By the time of Jane Austen (1775–1817), journalist/historian Anne Scott-James points out, "There were plenty of minor gentry, on social terms with the squire and the parson, living in cottages and gardening with the same amateur skill and delight they brought to music, sketching and literature." Austen was among them, living with her mother and sister in a redbrick cottage in the Hampshire village of Chawton in the latter part of her life.

George Eliot's fictional miniseries, *Scenes of Clerical Life*, published in the 1850s, includes a memorable passage describing the laissez-faire, cottage-style approach to productive gardening, which already seemed to be disappearing

← In *The Artist's Garden at Vetheuil*, 1881, Claude Monet (1840–1926) distilled the carefree essence of cottage garden style at his home beside the river Seine. He called it "a ravishing spot," populated with towering sunflowers in high summer.

→→ The garden of horticulturist Sarah Cook sees spring turn into summer illuminated by her National Collection of Cedric Morris irises [page 79] and vivid scarlet *Tulipa sprengeri*.

→ George Eliot's elegiac depiction of an old vicarage garden praised its succession of old-fashioned flowers among edibles destined for the kitchen.

TOP ROW
— Sweet williams
— Heirloom kale 'Dwarf Green Curled'
— Annual poppies

MIDDLE ROW
— Gooseberries, *Ribes uva-crispa*
— Moss rose, 'William Lobb'
— Ripening red currants

BOTTOM ROW
— Apple blossom
— Orange tiger lily, *Lilium lancifolium*
— Bearded bellflower, *Campanula barbata*

by the mid-nineteenth century. New inventions, rapidly increasing mechanization, and prosperity had led to the development of affordable conservatories. These, in turn, were able to nurture an influx of bold and unusual plants imported from warmer climates. New plants required novel thinking on how best to display them, not just in the grandest gardens but also the smaller grounds of the expanding middle classes of professionals and industrialists. Seasonal, temporary displays were all the rage, set out in geometric patterns and formal rows. In contrast, Eliot's elegiac depiction of an old vicarage garden reminds us how the unpretentious charm and uplifting nature of cottage-style, productive planting was receding in the rapidly developing industrial age. She also identifies numerous species that had long been cherished in much more modest gardens: those productive patches attached to rural cottages.

> The garden was one of those old-fashioned paradises which hardly exist any longer except as memories of our childhood: no finical separation between flower and kitchen garden there; no monotony of enjoyment for one sense to the exclusion of another; but a charming paradisiacal mingling of all that was pleasant to the eyes and good for food. The rich flower-border running along every walk, with its endless succession of spring flowers, anemones, auriculas, wall-flowers, sweet-williams, campanulas, snapdragons, and tiger-lilies, had its taller beauties, such as moss and Provence roses, varied with espalier apple-trees. The crimson of a carnation was carried out in the lurking crimson of the neighboring strawberry-beds; you gathered a moss-rose one moment and a bunch of currants the next; you were in a delicious fluctuation between the scent of jasmine and the juice of gooseberries. Then what a high wall at one end, flanked by a summer-house so lofty, that after ascending its long flight of steps you could see perfectly well there was no view worth looking at.

Cottage gardens are often very personal creations, but early examples were much humbler than that described by Eliot, having evolved out of necessity, to provide families with homegrown produce, some healing herbs, and maybe

seasonal flowers in the days long before the availability of supermarkets, florists, and greengrocers.

In this book, photographer Marianne Majerus and I want to share our enthusiasm for creating "cottage garden abundance" at home, with the inspirational guidance of gardens both great and small. The present surge of interest in homesteading and the "cottagecore" aesthetic is not merely nostalgia but also a practical lifestyle choice. Today's gardeners are concerned with traceability, "food miles," and health reasons—such as the known physical and mental health benefits of planting and tending a garden. There is also, of course, the undoubted sense of achievement and enjoyment linked to growing, using, and sharing homegrown produce.

We have therefore set out some brief scene-setting and historical background, although the greater focus of this book is looking forward, with plenty of visual inspiration. Individual chapters profile seasonal flowers, herbs and salads, vegetables, fruit, and a handy guide to some key plant varieties to attract those most welcome and tireless workers: the pollinators. Trees, hedges, and topiary are important players in the overall living framework, bringing height, scale, shade, privacy, or character, as well as vital habitat for birds and other creatures. Alongside the joy of growing plants, pictorial sections spotlight ideas for sympathetic use of structural materials that enhance a gentle cottage garden ambience and a look at creative ways to bring water into the garden.

Today, as so many people are returning in droves to growing at least some of their own food, new generations of adventurous gardeners are appreciating the advantages. Modern-day cottage gardening, like its venerable earlier incarnations, embraces the natural world, while reaping the rewards of productivity and personal accomplishment.

← Square stepping stones form discreet access paths between the flowers and vegetables in this attractive productive garden, including onions, lettuces, sweet williams *Dianthus barbatus* 'Sweet Mixed', margined by peach and golden-leaved heuchera and old-fashioned roses.

→→ Delicate beeblossom *Gaura (Oenothera) lindheimeri* and purple coneflower *Echinacea purpurea* stand out against the ferny foliage of *Artemisia* 'Silver Queen'.

Your aim, or one of your aims, is to suggest a "paradise" in the terms of the elements already existing on the site and which give it its special character, to intensify and concentrate the *genius loci* and give free rein to a love of nature by offering each plant the best conditions possible for its development.

RUSSELL PAGE

1 · The Product of "Hands and Brains"

← Early summer pastels, with love-in-a-mist *Nigella damascena*, foxgloves, and *Rosa* 'Ispahan' joined by tall bearded irises 'Quaker Lady', 'Jane Phillips', and 'Black Douglas', at Hemingford Grey, Cambridgeshire.

WHAT IS A COTTAGE GARDEN? FIRST, WE MIGHT AS WELL ASK, WHAT is a cottage? These days, the net can be cast far and wide to answer that question, but the term is derived from the Middle English word *cottar*, referring to the period post-1066, after the successful Norman invasion of the British Isles by William the Conqueror. The conquest subdued the Anglo-Saxon population and increased the peasant class of agricultural workers living under the feudal system of Norman rule. "Cottars" lived in servitude, usually in cramped, humble dwellings in return for working on the land of the Norman overlords. Sometimes, there was a patch of land attached, but more frequently the open field system prevailed, whereby a narrow strip of land was made available to the cottar to grow food for his own family's consumption, alongside the manorial lord's crops and pastures.

John Woodforde, a twentieth-century journalist, was an indefatigable researcher into unsung histories of human enterprise, delving into topics as varied as the history of false teeth, bicycles, bricks, and wigs, to name but a few. His study of pre-twentieth-century cottage life, *The Truth About Cottages: A History and an Illustrated Guide to 50 Types of English Cottage*, candidly summed up the grim reality of the dwellings endured by many of the rural and agricultural poor in medieval times and later in Britain. He noted "a monotonous catalogue of scabrous floors, heaps of ordure, open sewers, polluted wells and windows stuffed with rags."

Somewhat more engagingly, he also traced the diverse architectural styles that developed regionally across half a millennium, from the early Tudors onward. According to the key natural building materials readily at hand in each locality, a cottage could be built from limestone, sandstone, timber, chalk, clay (used for brickmaking), or cob (a blend usually of clay and sand subsoils, mixed with straw and water), for example. Likewise, architect Christopher Powell observed, "The rich variety of cottages is a reason for their powerful appeal. Most looked diverse when new and have grown more so with age. Hands and brains were what once fashioned all cottages, no matter what may have altered them since."

←← The thatched Clergy House at Alfriston, East Sussex, sits between the village green and tranquil water meadows. Built circa 1400, the six-hundred-year-old-cottage was the first property to be taken on by the National Trust, in 1896. Its cottage garden includes many roses, productive beds, and an ancient orchard.

While the open field system had long been widely adopted, the cottage garden is understood to have developed when the Black Death (bubonic plague) of the mid-fourteenth century receded. Although figures are uncertain, the plague is thought to have claimed the lives of perhaps up to half the population of Europe and the British Isles, particularly affecting the rural poor, who were already undernourished and often living in dangerously unsanitary conditions. Loss of population cascaded into a situation where there was plenty of land to spare but extreme workforce shortages. This situation enabled the working cottage dweller, if not actually to "call the shots," to at least have a chance at demanding better terms from a manorial landlord. The cottar might negotiate to have a small personal plot made available beside his house, for example, instead of a designated slender strip somewhere in the common land, or among the landlord's open fields.

So, the early cottage garden appeared and evolved. It was certainly a place of utility and necessity, probably with a few incidental flowers, but subdued in color, when compared with modern images of cottage gardening. While details are somewhat scarce, strands of information filter through the medieval writings

→ The nineteenth-century decorator William Morris declared Bibury, in the Cotswolds, "The most beautiful village in England." Its medieval wool store was converted into these weavers' cottages in the seventeenth century. Morris and others, including *Country Life* magazine, nostalgically celebrated rural cottage life.

of, for instance, Geoffrey Chaucer, via his rustic *The Canterbury Tales*. In "The Nun's Priest's Tale," Chaucer tells us about a poor, elderly widow and her two daughters who live in a simple cottage with a dark interior, further blackened by soot from a smoky fire. The widow has a modest dairy enterprise, and her patch of land is a sort of smallholding, containing seven chickens and a rooster, three pigs, three cows, and a lone sheep. This might suggest that the family was better off—or at any rate, better fed—than many of the rural poor, having some access to eggs, milk, butter, and meat, but Chaucer advises us that their diet is chiefly dark bread and milk.

A yeerd she hadde, enclosed al aboute
With stikkes, and a drye dych withoute.

The widow's garden is enclosed all around, by a pale, or palisade, fence set alongside the edge of a ditch, a popular medieval method of penning livestock.

↑ The Victorian gardening expert Gertrude Jekyll (p. 141) studied and promoted the preservation of ancient vernacular homes, typified by Valewood Farmhouse, near Haslemere. In the 1920s, she supplied its owner with traditional cottage garden plants from her Munstead Wood nursery a few miles up the road.

It contains a selection of medicinal herbs, including centaury, fumitory, and ground ivy (*Glechoma hederacea*) and a number of species that would be regarded as highly toxic today. Loose-leaved cabbages, known as "wortes," or coleworts, were an important part of the early medieval diet, and they make an appearance in "The Nun's Priest's Tale"; presumably these and other edibles and herbs were set apart from the widow's grazing livestock.

In the time of the Tudors, and particularly from the reign of Queen Elizabeth I onward, overseas explorations and exchanges of plants with other countries rapidly broadened the choice of species grown in the British Isles. Shakespeare's plays and poems reference some of them, while his contemporary, John Gerard, described the properties of many more in his *Herball*, first published in 1597.

Plant exploration and exchange has continued ever since, of course, and sometimes the humble cottage garden has benefited. A very large number of formal, geometric gardens surrounding England's finer houses were swept away during the eighteenth century to be replaced by the grass and trees of landscaped parks. In one way or another, many of the exotic bulbs and flowers of the earlier gardens found their way into the gardens of nearby cottages; cuttings taken from roses and fragrant shrubs took root and enhanced the humble homes.

Over time, the cottage garden became a much more visually interesting and appealing place than in Chaucer's day. The "hands and brains" responsible for fashioning homes out of immediately local materials also created gardens of utility and considerable charm. By the mid-nineteenth century, well-heeled city dwellers in the expanding middle classes were searching out country cottages for rural weekending, relaxation, and entertaining, away from the urban smoke and grime. Likewise, the cottage garden, enthusiastically promoted by gardener-publisher William Robinson (1838–1935), became a desirable diversion and also something to be painted, in what came to be known as the "chocolate box" style. Numerous artists contemporary with Robinson developed a specialty in the genre, among the most successful of whom were Myles Birket Foster, George Samuel Elgood, and Helen Allingham.

← Artist George S. Elgood (1851–1943) painted *Cleeve Prior: Sunflowers* in 1901. Gertrude Jekyll admired its "narrow grass paths bordered with old-fashioned flowers" including dahlias, lavenders, Michaelmas daisies, "and sweet herbs for the kitchen."

→→ The view from the potato patch: A typically charming cottage garden, with euphorbias and summer-flowering *Phygelius aequalis* 'Yellow Trumpet', plus lavenders, roses, and foxgloves.

↑ From the mid-nineteenth century, relaxed cottage garden plants became fashionable in the gardens of much grander houses. Here, hollyhocks dominate at Blyborough, Lincolnshire, with crown daisies *Chrysanthemum coronarium*, pansies, erigeron, and pink phlox.

Part of the great heritage of the cottage garden is as a repository for novelty plants that might otherwise have disappeared. "Florist" societies emerged in the seventeenth and eighteenth centuries, chiefly among wealthy amateurs who formed clubs with special interests in flowers such as the Asian *Ranunculus*, in its many forms and hues. Primroses were collected under the heading of *polyanthus*, referring to the kinds with multiple flowers arranged on a single stalk, while the display of remarkable *Primula auricula* hybrids was a hobby among the nobility. A mania for collecting special tulips made and lost fortunes for some people. Later, when prices dropped and these once rare and expensive flowers became more commonplace, they were taken up with enthusiasm among cottage gardeners who formed their own clubs for showing and sharing these special blooms.

In the second quarter of the twenty-first century, we have at our disposal an extraordinary range of plant material drawn from around the world, bred by both amateur gardeners and specialist nurseries. Alongside developments aimed at perfecting size or visual characteristics, plant breeders have focused on aspects of weather tolerance, disease resistance, or flower longevity, among other things.

The following pages showcase many examples of relaxed, cottage-style planting in a modern idiom. Color theming with perennials and annuals is perhaps again as popular as it was when discussed by artist-gardener Gertrude Jekyll (1843–1932) at the end of the nineteenth century, or by Canadian nursery owners Nori and Sandra Pope in the last quarter of the twentieth. Although one cannot be too prescriptive (and of course, there are many exceptions), current ornamental planting styles tend to be "shaggier" than their equivalents just a generation or two ago. Grasses of many kinds are popular and frequently incorporated into cottage-style borders as well as designs inspired by meadows.

Where kitchen gardening is concerned, one of the biggest trends for modern cottage gardeners is the widespread adoption of raised beds, which have numerous advantages (page 196). For anyone not especially DIY minded, there is a huge range of easily assembled modular kits available, including hardwood and softwood timbers, woven willow panels, and powder-coated metal, such as preformed corrugated sheets. As well as making crop cultivation much easier, they have a rustic, country garden ambience that does not take up much space.

Another major development of recent times is the broad choice of compact plant varieties and seeds for staples including cucumbers, peppers, tomatoes, and squashes of various kinds. They have enabled worthwhile harvests of container-grown food, even on patios and balconies. Conversely, greater awareness of heritage edibles is ensuring continued access to long-cherished varieties. Many have superior taste and texture, but they could have other characteristics that are unappealing to commercial growers. For example, an old and delicious heritage tomato that crops up gradually, over a long period, or lacks uniformity in presentation, is less useful to the commercial grower, but those very characteristics make the tomatoes appealing to the home gardener.

→→ At Alfriston Clergy House, East Sussex, the medieval cottage is glimpsed beyond a high yew hedge, which gives shelter to the modest productive garden. Its relaxed atmosphere is carefully retained, with flowers such as *Lavatera* and nasturtiums growing among the vegetables.

2 · The Ancient Art of Topiary

TOPIARY, THE TECHNIQUE OF USING SHEARS TO SHAPE ALL MANNER of trees and shrubs into crafted forms, is a horticultural art that has been cherished for centuries. For its creator, there is the satisfaction of seeing the intended forms develop over time. Topiary also creates unintrusive "soft sculpture" in the natural greens and textures of nature. It can be deployed as an eye-catching focal point, or perhaps to lead the eye along a series of creations, regular or irregular. Simple shapes, such as balls, cubes, and pyramids are easy to create; you just need to have sharp shears in hand and keep picturing your intended result as you cut. Confidence is gained with practice! There are also ready-made wire frameworks widely available from garden stores and online, for easily creating anything from simple geometry to birds and quite complicated animals, very much maintaining the cottage garden tradition.

Although birds and animals have long been popular subjects for the gardener's shears, tiered "wedding cake" or cartwheel designs go way back, as can sometimes be seen in medieval illustrations. In Edwardian country gardens, a hedge top decorated with a clipped green fox and hounds was seen from time to time, while peacock designs were popular particularly in Victorian and Edwardian gardens, in both the pleasure garden of the manor house and the front yard of the humble cottage.

Topiary goes back even further, of course, for the Romans are believed to have brought their topiary ideas to Britain nearly two millennia ago. We know from various contemporary writers and archaeological discoveries that the *topiarius*, the gardener creating such work, was both skilled and imaginative, working in myrtle, box, bay laurel, and cypress, as well as training ivy.

Topiary is also a very long established part of formal garden making in Northern Europe, particularly in France, Belgium, Italy, and the Netherlands. In the United States, the early colonial settlers established a tradition of boxwood (*Buxus sempervirens*) and yew (*Taxus baccata*) topiary, directly brought from the British Isles (see Colonial Williamsburg, page 41).

An interesting transatlantic connection with the past can be seen in one of England's finest topiary gardens, which was owned for forty years by the

← Emerald waves: At Theobald's Farmhouse, Middlesex, exemplary knot patterns in boxwood are punctuated by contrasting topiary pyramids in variegated box. A wedding-cake tree, 'Variegata', catches the retreating sunlight.

→→ A traditional Derbyshire cottage, resplendent with traditional topiaries in yew (*Taxus baccata*). Yew naturally prefers limestone areas and freely draining ground. Sometimes cottage garden topiaries of this type are centuries old.

↑ Deciduous trees can make excellent topiary, changing their foliage colors through the seasons. Here, hornbeam (*Carpinus betulus*), beech (*Fagus sylvatica*), and copper beech with bronze-plum foliage, guide the eye, underplanted with 'Ballerina' tulips.

American decorator and socialite Nancy Lancaster (1897–1994). Haseley Court, in Oxfordshire, her last home, has a remarkable garden of topiaries that appear to be chess pieces, laid out on a broad, flat lawn. That particular arrangement dates from a replanting in about 1850, but topiary was already a feature there much earlier, as it was in many other grand gardens of the Tudor period. In 1540 the antiquary John Leland noted the fair walks, topiary, orchards, and pools at Little Haseley. Lancaster put more topiary into her redesigned walled garden, including a wagon wheel, designed as if laid flat, with earth areas for planting between the "spokes." She also edged the garden's beds with low box hedging, infilling with cottage garden flowers and old-fashioned roses. The ensemble reminded her of the old gardens of Virginia, where she had spent her childhood among the state's historic boxwood gardens. Oxfordshire itself, and nearby Gloucestershire, are rich in village cottage gardens with topiary. The belt of Cotswold limestone that underpins that region yields an alkaline soil that is enjoyed by box and yew,

↑ Onward and upward: Stepped box topiary flanks a small brick stairway, lending a touch of grandeur and confirming the topiarist's mastery of both shears and proportions.

so a country tradition of charming topiary has existed there for an unknown number of centuries.

Recent years have seen boxwood plants devastated by a widespread box blight fungal disease, as well as attacks from the caterpillar of a particular moth, *Cydalima perspectalis*. A lot of research has been done to combat these problems, particularly in the Netherlands, where box hedging is a deeply embedded part of the country's gardening traditions. A fertilizer known as Topbuxus has recently been specifically developed to help plants recover from the stress of the blight disease; I have heard good reports of its efficacy.

The caterpillars can be very difficult to control, since multiple hatchings may be hard to spot in time. A bad infestation can strip a plant or substantial part of a hedge quite bare within a matter of days. Certain strains of the naturally occurring soil-borne bacterium, known as *Bacillus thuringiensis* (Bt), have been the basis of box moth control by professional growers for some time, but in some places are not available to amateur gardeners. Alternative plant choices can be the best

↑ Carved wooden faces confirm the charming nature of these neat little boxwood sheep.

→ Playful topiary has delighted and inspired gardeners for centuries.

solution. They certainly save the worry of moth infestations as well as negating any need to apply control measures several times through the growing season. Among them, *Ilex crenata*, a dense and very small-leaved Japanese holly, is one of the best box alternatives, best suited to a neutral to slightly acidic soil. *Lonicera nitida*, sometimes called boxwood honeysuckle, is fairly unfussy about soil type. It clips well and has very small leaves but grows rapidly, requiring trimming three or more times a year to maintain a good outline. A number of dwarf hebe varieties have a naturally rounded shape, good for the "box ball" look; Hebe 'Emerald Green Globe' is a compact example and also makes a nice container subject. Native to New Zealand, some hebes are not completely frost hardy, so it depends upon where you live whether these are a good choice for you.

EVERGREENS FOR TOPIARY

Numerous evergreens can be turned into topiary. Here is a short list to creative cutting. Choose small-leaved species for little topiaries and where fiddly details are required, for best effect. Large-leaved species such as camellias, laurels, and holm oaks are most effective when used for large specimens of simple shape.

- *Buxus sempervirens*, box
- *Camellia* × *williamsii*, hybrid camellia
- *Cupressus arizonica*, Arizona cypress
- *Elaeagnus* × *ebbingei*
- *Euonymus japonicus*, Japanese Euonymus
- *Euonymus microphyllus*, box-leaved Euonymus
- *Hebe rakaiensis*
- *Hebe topiaria*
- *Ilex aquifolium*, common holly
- *Ilex crenata*, Japanese holly
- *Laurus nobilis*, bay laurel
- *Ligustrum delavayanum* (jonandrum) Delavay privet
- *Lonicera nitida*, boxwood honeysuckle
- *Luma apiculata*, Chilean myrtle
- *Myrtus communis*, myrtle
- *Phillyrea angustifolia*
- *Pittosporum tenuifolium*
- *Prunus lusitanica*, cherry laurel
- *Quercus ilex*, holm or holly oak
- *Taxus baccata*, yew
- *Taxus cuspidata*, Japanese yew
- *Thuja occidentalis* 'Smaragd', arborvitae

Tuberoses and Tobacco

← The picturesque charm of Colonial Williamsburg's eighteenth-century houses is further enhanced by splendid topiary and neat picket fences.

COVERING SOME THREE HUNDRED ACRES, COLONIAL WILLIAMSBURG is a remarkable "living history" museum, comprising the restored eighteenth-century colonial capital of Virginia. Its network of thoroughfares and side streets contains several hundred restored and re-created buildings, presenting a picturesque and interesting little town. As well as its grander public buildings, such as the Governor's Palace, Capitol, and Courthouse, there are numerous historic houses and pretty cottages with sturdy, brick chimney stacks. They line up along the streets, behind appealing restored gardens in the formal styles of the period. These productive plots, with brick-edged and box-margined beds, are accessed via narrow brick paths; the contents of their beds have much in common with country cottage gardens of their contemporaries in England and the Low Countries, for they contain a mixture of vegetables, ornamental flowers, herbs, fruit, and topiary.

More than forty gardens and green spaces can be explored and, as part of its focus on keeping Williamsburg's colonial history alive, special attention is paid to collecting and growing heritage varieties of flowers and edibles, with the gardeners carrying out their tasks while wearing period costumes.

One of the more exotic flowers that grew in some of the Williamsburg gardens in colonial days is the tuberose, *Polianthes tuberosa* (also known as *Agave amica*), bearing spikes of trumpetlike, white, waxy flowers. In the evening, they put out a strong, intensely spicy-floral scent that has been used in perfumery since the seventeenth century. Native to Mexico and growing from bulblike tubers with brittle, fleshy roots, the Williamsburg tuberoses are grown in clay pots, so they can be moved indoors over the winter months.

In about 1736, Peter Collinson (1694–1768), an English merchant, gardener, and botanist of note, sent bulbs of tuberose to Williamsburg dignitary and keen gardener John Custis IV, whose four-acre plot became one of the finest gardens in the American colonies at that time. The two plant collectors exchanged numerous letters, roots, and seeds over more than ten years. Collinson's letter, attached to the tuberoses, advised:

←← In early spring, before the big trees expand their leaves, it is possible to gain views across Williamsburg's historic streets, above the neat boxwood hedges.

↓ To maintain a green carpet throughout the quieter months, ivy is used to infill the beds as neat ground cover, enhancing the greenery of mature yew topiary. As spring progresses, daffodils emerge here and there.

> 6 · Tuberoses – att the Approach of Winter take
> these up and Lay the Roots singly to Dry in a Roome,
> when well Dry'd putt them in straw in a Roome where you
> keep a Constant Fire. In the spring as soone as the severe
> Frosts are over plant them in the ground.

The Mexican single-flowered tuberose is considered an heirloom flower of the colonial period, thanks to its association with the old gardens. Probably it scented many of them, as people swapped roots and cuttings of their cherished plants with family and friends.

In Virginia, however, evening fragrance is also closely associated with the tobacco plant, which, from its early colonial days, was the region's most successful cash crop. While the Indigenous tribes introduced English settlers to the rather dark and bitter *Nicotiana rustica*, by 1612 seeds of the milder *Nicotiana tabacum* had been obtained, which became the European standard for commercial production. As a key part of its agricultural history, tobacco continues to be grown at Colonial Williamsburg, perfuming the evenings with its sweet fragrance when the tubular, pale pink flowers are in bloom.

In cottage gardens, tobacco plants have long been popular, providing sweetly scented summer sparkle. The aforementioned *Nicotiana rustica*, also known as

Aztec tobacco, was grown and admired by the doyenne of cottage gardening, Margery Fish (1892–1969), who said "its little green flowers are delightful." More popular today are the tall, white-flowered *N. sylvestris* (woodland tobacco), which has a notable sweet scent and numerous shorter hybrids, flowering in a range of shades, including lime green, that fit well into small gardens and patio pots. Grow tobacco as a half-hardy annual, from seeds or plug plants, in good quality potting soil.

↖↑ Two heritage flowers perfume the night air in summer, attracting moths as pollinators: the spicy-floral scented Mexican tuberose *Polianthes tuberosa* (left), and commercial tobacco, *Nicotiana tabacum* (right).

3 · Paths and Paving

TRADITIONALLY, A COTTAGE GARDEN PATH IS STRAIGHT, PROVIDING the most direct route from A to B: from the lane to the doorway, whether the door is located on the front of the house or tucked away in a side elevation.

"The point of a path is to be able to walk dryshod in wet weather and to have a firm footing," said Russell Page. "Paths of gravel, sand, tan, bark or stone chippings must have a firm foundation and one which will quickly drain away surplus water. But all these materials need a great deal of maintenance." He suggested carefully rolling gravel paths into a foundation layer of tarmac to maintain its effect for years without needing further upkeep and recommended this treatment for kitchen gardens. "Paths are all-important. They should lead as directly as possible from place to place and should not be made where they are not necessary . . . I know of nothing that makes a garden more forlorn than an unused path."

Except in some of the immediate environs of her Edwin Lutyens–built house, famed gardener Gertrude Jekyll left her numerous (and well-trodden) garden paths unpaved, preferring to walk on the earth itself, between the borders of seasonal flowers and in the plant nursery area. It was a deliberate choice and part of her attachment to the natural ways of the countryside; yet it was easy enough to have earthen paths in her part of Surrey, where the ground is comprised of light and freely draining, sandy soil. During and after heavy rain, it does not churn up into a muddy quagmire as heavy, water-retentive soils are inclined to do.

Jekyll did, however, take great interest in the paving she saw used in the old cottages around her. She observed in the old country dwellings by the roadsides, made with whatever materials were close at hand: "Often there are a few square yards of paving at a cottage entrance, and most commonly some of the same sandstone slabs are laid flat, and the rest of the pavement is a 'pitching' of the black stones that are found in and near the heathlands just below the surface. They are water-washed stones containing a large proportion of iron . . . an admirable paving surface; they are so hard that their wearing power is almost indefinite."

←← A relaxed old country garden with simple topiary and a hierarchy of paving: Random-sized flagstones lead in a straight line away from the doorway. Ancillary paths of pea gravel enable access on either side, in a less formal manner.

← A dapple-shaded path of stepping stones and gravel leads the way through pink Astrantia, ferns, box balls, and *Hydrangea arborescens*.

→→ Curvy contours: A contemporary take on crazy paving. Irregular flagstones and mellow brickwork lead between curved walls of local flint stone, with pockets for planting campanula and other flowers here and there.

→ Walk this way: Varied treatments for paths in small spaces.

TOP ROW
— Herringbone brickwork margined with ferns and *Hakonechloa macra*
— Granite stepping stones
— Timber path at Le Jardin de Berchigranges

MIDDLE ROW
— Stepping stones and sea-washed pebbles
— Salami slices of logs at Le Jardin de Berchigranges
— Stepping stones lead across a lawn at Barnsley House

BOTTOM ROW
— Secure stones cross a pond
— Random-sized flagstones, margined with brick and 'Hidcote' lavender
— Chunky stone and timber steps with self-sown erigeron daisies

→→ A diamond patterned path of stone setts and gravel terminates with an old millstone at York Gate, Yorkshire.

A traditional Surrey cottage might be furnished by the door with a mixed pavement of sandstone slabs, sandstone pieces, dark ironstones, and, for good measure, some clay bricks. The materials were not only picturesque, creating varied patterns and colors in the paving, they were immediately at hand, borne from the very same ground, and the perfect foil for cottage garden flowers flopping over the edges.

A fashion for garden "crazy paving" (whereby unevenly shaped and sized pieces of flat stone are laid to create an informal pattern) flourished during Jekyll's period of influence and can be seen in many gardens of the Arts and Crafts period. Contemporary luminaries such as Edwin Lutyens, Harold Peto, Harry Tipping, and Oliver Hill, among others, employed this style. It remained in vogue for decades and can be seen sometimes with a circular millstone dropped into the design, as Lutyens did for Jekyll at Munstead Wood in the 1890s.

Crazy paving has a much earlier provenance, however, going back at least to ancient Rome and has turned up in Romano-British excavations. Page was circumspect about its modern usage. "The *opus incertum* of the Romans, where irregular slabs of stone or lava are carefully fitted together with the narrowest possible joints, have great beauty if only because one senses the skill of the craftsman whose feeling for, and handling of, stone remains as long as his pavement exists. To drop a mass of small bits of stone and set them where they fall, and then to fill the intervening spaces with grass or rock plants, gives a restless appearance and makes a great deal of work."

Today, crazy paving is enjoying a revival among garden and landscape designers after several decades of being outmoded. Its current resurgence probably has as much to do with environmental benefits as aesthetic considerations. Crazy paving can use up recycled materials, "waste" stone, and leftover pieces since precision measurements are not required for its assembly. It also has a rustic appeal that suits cottage-style plants, as Jekyll observed, enhancing a contemporary cottage ambience. Interesting treatments can be seen among the range of exemplary paving shown in this section.

4 · The Vitality of Spring

March comes in like a lion and goes out like a lamb
April showers bring May flowers
Ne'er cast a clout till May be out
Oak before ash, in for a splash; ash before oak, in for a soak
Spring is sooner recognized by plants than by men

IN THE TEMPERATE NORTHERN HEMISPHERE, SPRING PROBABLY enjoys "the lion's share" of season- and weather-focused proverbs, some of them directly plant related, as in the ancient saying regarding oak and ash trees. (For a long time, it was used to predict the weather in the coming months, based upon which of these two trees opened its new foliage first.) That the season is "sooner recognized by plants than by men" is more easily justified, for plants respond naturally to the lengthening days, their sap running freely as temperatures start to rise and the soil warms.

"Now I expect great things of March, and I don't often get them," wrote a fixture of cottage flower gardening, Margery Fish (page 67). "Just as we know that February means rain, we fear a certain amount of bluster in March. There have been years when we've had sunshine and warmth in this month, but not often. We ought to be able to enjoy the daffodils which come up in their hundreds, but so often there's a fiendish east wind waiting to smite round every corner, sometimes keen frosts and even snow can spoil all enjoyment in the garden and ruin the fresh beauty of the flowers, but luckily that is not usual." Fish neatly sums up the absolute capriciousness of the season.

There is an urgency to spring and an unparalleled vitality as every day reveals incremental change. The very earliest wild primroses—a cottage garden classic—can start to appear precociously, one here, one there, arriving with the new year; but as spring unfolds they carpet any ground that suits them, in a wash of creamy-yellow blooms, sometimes joined by other tints. They sit well in the company of forget-me-nots, bluebells, or the self-spreading, dainty *Tulipa bakeri* 'Lilac Wonder', beckoning roving bees.

← Round-leaved Alexanders (*Smyrnium rotundifolium*), prettily joined by *Lunaria annua*, also known as honesty, or "the money plant," due to its silvery, round seedpods resembling coins.

→→ A tapestry of early spring purple and gold: *Crocus vernus* and the wild daffodil, *Narcissus pseudonarcissus*, naturalized in the grass at Great Dixter, East Sussex.

→ The sights and scents of spring, via bulbs and wildflowers.

TOP ROW

— The cowslip, *Primula veris*

— *Anemone blanda* and its variety 'White Splendour'

— *Muscari armeniacum* 'Big Smile' explored by a honeybee

MIDDLE ROW

— Primroses, *Primula vulgaris*

— *Helleborus* x *hybridus* 'Pale Picotee'

— Assorted dainty daffodils

BOTTOM ROW

— Hen-and-chickens daisy, *Bellis perennis* 'Prolifera'

— *Scilla (Chionodoxa) luciliae*

— Wallflower, *Erysimum* 'Sunset Purple'

Daffodils and tulips carry the season in a multitude of ways, filling terra-cotta pots with bright colors or naturalized in grass, perhaps among blossoming trees. By choosing early-, mid-season, and late-season tulips, the parade of color (and in some cases, scent) is uplifting, whatever the weather. Some orange-flowered tulips, particularly the elegant, lily-flowered *Tulipa* 'Ballerina', seem to be particularly good at wafting a delicious, sherbet-vanilla fragrance in their vicinity.

From late winter onward through spring it is hellebore season. Double-flowered varieties have been raised in many colorways over recent years, and very pretty they are. Nevertheless, the simplicity of single-flowered *Helleborus* × *hybridus*, in its multitude of colors, can be difficult to improve upon. Bees love visiting the slightly nodding flowers of hellebores with their neat rosette of nectaries and prominent anthers; in foraging over the flowers, the bees assist natural cross-pollination that sometimes creates interesting, unplanned hybrids.

Mid-spring is also the moment for erythroniums, the dainty dog's tooth violets. They carpet the ground with marbled foliage topped by swept-back parasols of flowers in whites, pinks, and yellows in great abundance once established. These shade lovers relish the sort of ground also enjoyed by camellias and rhododendrons: fertile, humus-rich, and slightly acidic soil, which is not boggy, but never gets too dry, either.

For the gardener, spring begins, of course, in the previous autumn, when the work is put in, planting bulbs: daffodils, miniature irises, Muscari, scillas, tulips, and probably much else besides. Also, perhaps, the planting of new shrubs and trees to bloom among them: laburnum, camellia, magnolia, lilac, weigela, cherry, crab apple, and plum. Spring is their moment to perform, the blossoms and bulbs exploding in a floral fantasia.

Fragrant lilacs have their moment in mid-spring, bearing panicles of tiny cross-shaped flowers, not just in their original "lilac" hue, but in crimson, purple, pink, white, cream, and near yellow and with complex double-flowered varieties as well. They waft delicious scent for yards around.

Ribes sanguineum is the beloved flowering currant of traditional cottage gardens. It never disappoints through April, bearing generous clusters of strawberry-red flowers explored by bees attracted to the pungent scent in both flower and leaf. It was the nineteenth-century explorer David Douglas who exported the flowering currant to the British Isles, having discovered it during his travels in America's Pacific Northwest nearly two hundred years ago.

Another hardy and dependable bloomer for mid-spring that I would not like to be without is the Amelanchier, known as snowy Mespilus or serviceberry, also native to North America—specifically, Canada. This is a tree that appears to be in a hurry. Its April flowers all open in rapid succession on still-bare stems and, just as quickly, they fall, like snow, within a few days, when the wind blows

through. By then, the leaves are already unfurling; they are coppery-colored at first, before rapidly shifting to bright green, while tiny fruits quickly emerge where the blossoms had been. By early May they have already become small pink berries that do not last long, since the birds—mainly blackbirds and wood pigeons hereabouts—gorge upon them until they are gone. It is a reminder that the nesting season is well underway; easily pecked fruits such as these are welcome energy revivers for parent birds who are busy, busy, busy all day, finding morsels for their ever-ravenous chicks.

Old-Fashioned Cottage Flowers

Traditional cottage garden flowers of the season include ground-hugging anemones such as the windflower *Anemone blanda*, with yellow-centered, daisy-like flowers of violet-blue, and the wood anemone, *A. nemorosa*, a native of deciduous forests across much of the Northern Hemisphere. It forms white carpets in the leaf litter, like drifts of snow, before any leaves unfurl in the tree canopy. John Gerard and John Parkinson, botanists of the Tudor period, cultivated brightly hued and double-flowered varieties of the wood anemone in the early seventeenth century, as well as the more familiar single blooms. Except where they were cherished in cottage gardens, humble anemones were out of fashion in the eighteenth and much of the nineteenth century. It was William Robinson who championed their revival, recommending them for the edges of borders, or as "ground plants" beneath shrubs.

The common daisy, *Bellis perennis*, used to be regarded as a weed of lawns, albeit a pretty one, with its tiny, yellow-centered flowers surrounded by a multitude of white ray petals. I remember childhood moments spent sitting on the grass with friends, making "daisy chains" into necklaces, bracelets, and head adornments, as has been done by countless generations of children across the Western world. No longer the lawn keeper's nightmare (except, understandably, on golf courses and bowling greens), the simple daisy is popular today as a cherished wildflower. The rural poet John Clare (1793–1864) celebrated the humble daisy with an admiring poem, beginning:

> The daisy is a happy flower
> That comes with early spring
> And brings with it the sunny hour
> When bees are on the wing.

Clare reminds us that simple daisies are useful early flowers for pollen-foraging insects. Elizabethan gardeners prized double-flowered forms bearing hundreds of petals per flower and in different colorways. Like the fancier forms of anemone, they survived by languishing in cottage gardens through subsequent centuries. Parkinson's 'Double fruitful Daisies or Jack-an-Apes on horsebacke' is better known by its cottage garden name, Hen-and-Chickens daisy, or the more botanical, *Bellis perennis* 'Prolifera'. This remarkable curiosity has somehow survived over the centuries; its main, dense flower head is parent to satellite "offspring" of miniature daisies, which spring directly out of the central flower.

Low walls and rocky places have long been ornamented with classic cottage plants such as *Alyssum saxatile* (also known as *Aurinia saxatilis*), which cascades in a springtime foam of tiny bright yellow flowers. It spreads easily and thrives in dry, sunny locations and stony crevices, often planted in the company of white-flowered *Arabis caucasica* (Snow on the Mountain) and the purple rock cress, *Aubrieta deltoidea*, the latter being available in a variety of jolly tints across the violet to red spectrum.

Wallflowers, Brompton stocks, Lady's smock (*Cardamine pratensis*), honesty (*Lunaria annua*), and sweet rocket (*Hesperis matronalis*) join *Alyssum*, *Arabis*, and *Aubrieta* as the "show-off" side of a large and agriculturally important family, the Brassicaceae. Their cousins, the cabbages and kales, broccoli and bok choy, watercress, mustard, radishes, and Brussels sprouts are all familiar candidates for the productive cottage garden; but it is their extrovert kin in the flower garden that invigorates the spring garden with so much vivacious color.

COTTAGE GARDEN BLOOMS IN SPRING

Bulbs

- *Allium spp.*, (many) mainly purples
- *Anemone*, inc. De Caen; wood anemone
- *Camassia*, Quamash; Indian hyacinth
- *Chionodoxa*, glory of the snow
- *Crocus* (many), wild species and cultivars
- *Fritillaria*, crown Imperial; snake's head fritillary
- *Hyacinthus*, (many) hyacinth, many shades
- *Iris*, dwarf bulb species and Dutch
- Muscari, (many), grape hyacinths
- *Narcissus*, (many) daffodils, in great variety
- *Scilla*, many, mainly blues to violet
- *Tulipa*, (many) Tulips in many shades, shapes, sizes

Annuals, biennials, perennials

- *Aquilegia vulgaris*, columbine; granny's bonnet
- *Arabis caucasica*, snow on the mountain
- *Aubrieta deltoidea*, rock cress
- *Bellis perennis* Flore Pleno, bachelor's buttons
- *Cheiranthus* and *Erysimum*, wallflower
- *Convallaria majalis*, lily of the valley
- *Doronicum*, leopard's bane
- *Erythronium*, dog's tooth violet
- *Euphorbia*, (many) spurge
- *Helleborus* × *hybridus*, hellebore
- *Iberis sempervirens*, candytuft
- *Lunaria annua*, honesty
- *Myosotis arvensis*, forget-me-not
- *Primula*, (many) inc. primrose, oxlip, cowslip
- *Ranunculus asiaticus*, Persian buttercup
- *Smyrnium perfoliatum*, perfoliate alexanders
- *Viola*, (many), inc. heartsease, pansy

Trees and Shrubs

- *Amelanchier lamarckii*, snowy mespilus
- *Camellia japonica, C.* × *williamsii*, camellia
- *Ceanothus spp.* Californian lilac
- Choisya 'Aztec Pearl', Mexican orange blossom
- *Cornus florida*, flowering dogwood
- *Forsythia* × *intermedia*, forsythia
- Laburnum × watereri 'Vossii', laburnum
- *Magnolia soulangeana, M. stellata*, Magnolia
- *Malus domestica*, apple tree (for blossom)
- *Malus sylvestris*, crab apple
- *Prunus avium*, wild cherry
- *Pyrus communis*, pear tree (blossom)
- *Ribes sanguineum*, flowering currant
- *Rosa* 'Canary Bird', Spring shrub rose
- *Syringa vulgaris*, lilac
- *Viburnum tomentosum*, Japanese snowball
- *Weigela florida*, weigela

Margery Fish

"IF MARCH HAS A FLOWER ALL ITS OWN I THINK IT IS THE DAFFODIL," wrote Margery Fish, outstanding gardener and indefatigable rescuer of old cottage garden/heritage flowers. "When we plant daffodils, I think we should observe how nature does the job. Wild daffodils grow in grass and usually in clumps, so that one can enjoy the outline of the flowers against a background of leaves."

Fish came late to gardening, but she made up for it with energetic determination, focus, and an engaging, unfussy writing style that rapidly garnered a captive audience. Her readers learned how an amateur in their own garden could create something beautiful in all seasons, despite little knowledge (albeit often supported by much perseverance).

Fish had already enjoyed an interesting twenty-year career in London's Fleet Street (the hub of all things journalistic) in the first half of the twentieth century. She found her niche with the *Daily Mail* newspaper, first as a secretarial assistant, in due course becoming secretary to the paper's proprietor, Lord Northcliffe, an enormously influential figure through the Edwardian age and the First World War. After the war, she was secretary to the editor, Walter Fish, whom she married in 1933.

Sensing that another war was in the cards, the couple bought the fifteenth-century stone house known as East Lambrook Manor, in Somerset, in 1937. "A poor battered old house that had to be gutted to be liveable, and a wilderness instead of a garden. . . . Redoing a house could be fun, but how would two Londoners go about the job of creating a garden from a farmyard and a rubbish heap?" she asked, in her first book, *We Made a Garden* (1956).

Walter Fish was a generation older than his wife and had a professional reputation for being somewhat autocratic and perfectionist. Likewise, his ideas about how to lay out the East Lambrook garden were very different from his wife's. Perhaps it is just as well that he died some years before *We Made a Garden* was published. It was compelling reading for postwar home gardeners, combining on-the-hoof practical experience (including her admitted mistakes) with recommendations of low-cost, easy flowers—and confessions of her own, and Walter's, opposing styles.

←← Zesty pots of tulips, including, from left: caramel and mahogany 'Bastia', red and gold lily-flowered 'Fly Away', pink and green parrot tulip 'Green Wave', fringed, dark burgundy 'Labrador', candy pink fringed 'Fancy Frills', mostly white 'Shirley'.

← The entrance to East Lambrook Manor, fifteenth-century-built home of Margery Fish, built from golden-hued local hamstone, a wonderful foil for garden plants. They include her own discovery, *Euphorbia characias* 'Lambrook Gold', *Centranthus ruber*, and an 'Albertine' rambler rose.

↑ Multitudes of herbaceous plants include variegated iris, phlomis, *Sisyrinchium striatum*, euphorbias, santolina, cottage garden pinks, and the meerkat-like spires of crimson loosestrife, *Lysimachia atropurpurea.*

On the topic of garden paths, "When it came to the job of making paths I discovered that this was a subject on which Walter had very strong views, and I had many lectures on how to achieve perfection." Regarding the lawn (which, together with the broad drive with plenty of car parking space, was Walter's pride and joy), "our lawn was taken right up to the high wall. I was grudgingly allowed a narrow bed in which to plant a few perennials and the climbers that were to clothe the wall, but I was warned that it was not to encroach too much on the precious green grass."

A succession of popular books followed, based on Margery Fish's experiences in the garden at East Lambrook and her rapidly expanded knowledge of plants, particularly forgotten flowers languishing in old cottage gardens. She wrote regular columns in the top selling journals *Amateur Gardening* and *Popular Gardening* in the 1950s and 1960s and was generous with both her knowledge and in sharing her plants. As a leading light in the horticultural world, she had many friends who shared a passion for plants; it is said that a tour of her three-quarters-of-an-acre garden could take up to five hours, as she pointed out the merits of this plant and that!

To some eyes, the Margery Fish style of garden—dominated by multitudes of herbaceous plants jostling with each other for ascendancy, or even survival, and flopping over narrow paths—could seem overpowering and almost confusing, in the height of summer abundance. Nevertheless, she had a keen eye for good form or character in each species. She championed, especially, those with interesting foliage, "silver-leaved" varieties and those with subtle tints or green flowers, such as hardy euphorbias and green-flowered hellebores.

Her discerning eye looked fairly at all the attributes of wildflowers as well as choicer garden selections. In *A Flower for Every Day*, one of her numerous popular books from the golden era of "plantsmanship" in the 1960s, hundreds of plants are considered and discussed, from snowdrops and forget-me-nots to humble buttercups. "I wonder why we fuss about double flowers, because on the whole I don't think they compare with the single-flowered forms. But many of them have the charm of the unusual. I wouldn't cherish an ordinary buttercup, however magnificent a specimen, but I check up regularly to see that no zealous friend has removed my precious double buttercups, which look just like common weeds when not in flower."

She was very fond of peonies, especially the simple, single-flowered kinds. "Early to flower is *Paeonia mlokosewitschii*, with its lovely single flowers. I have one complaint only to make about this lovely pale-yellow peony . . . and that is the short time the flowers stay with us. One waits all the year for those glorious globes of pale loveliness, but they come and go in less than a week; so much of one's enjoyment is anticipation but the foliage is good, turning crimson in autumn—and the bright cerise seedpods with black seeds are beautiful."

The fresh foliage of spring is at least as captivating and interesting as its flowers. There is a luminosity and energy in the season's new leaves, unfurling in a multitude of greens and, occasionally, alluring coppery tints.

← The crazy-paved path, lined with an avenue of *Chamaecyparis lawsoniana* 'Fletcheri' (Margery Fish called them her "pudding trees") and overflows of cottage garden flowers, including foxgloves, lilac-blue catmint *Nepeta* x *faasenii*, and scarlet *Salvia microphylla*.

5 · Arches, Arbors, Trellises

ARCHES, ARBORS, AND PERGOLAS PROVIDE TREMENDOUS OPPORTUNITIES to lift the garden literally into a different dimension. On a flat site, any of these features can be effective at elevating one's gaze, bringing an appearance of height and a focal point of interest—whether in the structure itself, or via the plants grown over it.

The garden arch and the pergola are made to walk under and through, so they should be located where it makes sense in the overall composition and have something interesting placed at the other end, to draw the eye and encourage exploration. A classic example was employed by Rosemary Verey at Barnsley House in Gloucestershire, whose famous wisteria and laburnum pergola concluded with a sundial and an implied invitation to further explore the garden. A carefully positioned bench also makes a good "destination" at the end of a pergola. Pergolas are especially associated with Mediterranean gardens, where the grapevine is the classic and adornment.

An ironwork tunnel has long been both a decorative garden feature and a vehicle on which to train plants, whether ornamental—such as roses—or edible,

← A classic and fragrant combination for spring strolls: Sweetly scented arches of fresh yellow laburnum and *Wisteria sinensis* underplanted with Dutch garlic *Allium hollandicum* 'Purple Sensation'.

↙ A trelliswork obelisk is a fine support for clematis 'Rhapsody'.

→→ An arched walk in the center of this kitchen garden is marked where the paths cross with the vigorous and abundantly flowering rose 'Veilchenblau'.

ONWARD AND UPWARD: HOW CLIMBERS CLIMB

When adorning a structure with climbing plants, it is necessary to consider what methods the plants use to achieve their upward inclination as they reach for height and light and provide support as necessary.

Spines

Except for the few spineless ones, climbing roses use their downturned thorns to hook onto convenient supports such as other plants, but when placed against a trellis or other structures, they need to be tied in as they grow.

Tendrils

Numerous plants use their modified stems, leaves, or leaf stalks to coil around canes to gain secure support during their upward trajectory. Grapevine, clematis, cucamelon, *Cobaea scandens* (cup-and-saucer vine), and sweet peas are among them. Virginia creeper takes ascendancy a step further, using its forked tendrils tipped with adhesive pads that allow the vine also to cling to smooth surfaces like walls and fences.

Twining stems

Wisterias, runner beans, and hops are classic twiners, rotating their shoot tips around any slender support close at hand, such as poles, canes, or trellis. Also, star jasmine (*Trachelospermum* spp.) and climbing honeysuckles. A plant as large and potentially unwieldy as wisteria requires pruning and tying in periodically, unless it is being allowed to clamber into the treetops.

Aerial roots

Climbing hydrangeas, trumpet vine (*Campsis radicans*), and ivy all develop short, clinging roots along their stems, gripping onto vertical surfaces, firmly anchoring them during their ascent, although some assistance may be needed for young plants until they are established.

such as apples or pears. All provide leafy shade to walk under in the peak of summer. Alternatively, tunnels make wonderful structures on which to grow fragrant sweet peas or seasonal curiosities, such as ornamental gourds.

Wooden trellis (known as "treillage" when it is especially sophisticated and decorative) is easily incorporated into arbors, arches, and pergola structures and is very attractive when painted in subtle or pastel tints. Any number of climbing plants sit well against such a backdrop; some will twine of their own accord while others need guidance and tying in as they grow.

Unlike the pergola and garden arch, which are structures to be passed through, the arbor or gazebo is a destination and therefore needs to offer some form of seating and probably a table for a book and a beverage or chairs for convivial conversation.

← Tepees made from wooden poles, such as hazel, enable sweet peas to twine their tendrils and climb

↖ A trellis makes a sturdy framework for the golden-leaved hop *Humulus lupulus* 'Aureus' to clamber over.

↑ The well-placed arbor or gazebo is a "destination," ideal for quiet contemplation or convivial conversation.

→→ A welcoming sight, *Rosa* 'Alchymist' frames the view to the house.

6 · The Abundance of Summer

ALLIUMS, FOXGLOVES, PEONIES, AND THE BEGINNINGS OF THE ROSES—these pretty blooms, joining the fresh greens of the season, make the early summer cottage garden an animated and optimistic place.

A level of uncertainty is baked in, however. Yes, uncertain, because the period of late May through June depends so much on how the weather of the previous weeks played out. A hot spell through spring, as sometimes happens, brings on some early summer flowers precociously and may even burn them up. (I have the spring of 2023 in mind, which was exceptional in parts of Britain.) Likewise, a prolonged cold or wet spring holds things back somewhat (as occurred in 2024!). Yet one way or another, everything is in irresistible growth mode and there is no stopping the energy of June, with lengthening days up to the solstice joined by warmer temperatures. Back in the 1950s, Margery Fish summed it up with this characteristic wry observation:

> June is the month that takes care of itself. Even the dullest garden can't help being colorful in June. When the cow parsley reaches shoulder level in the hedgerows and the roadside is scented with honeysuckle and wild roses, the garden too seems to grow up overnight. This is the time when one discovers if one has planted too closely, and I always have, and if one has staked sufficiently and efficiently, and I never have.
>
> June is the month when roses tumble over the walls, the tall spikes of delphiniums tower above the jungle of the borders, at the mercy of the gales that nearly always turn up some time in June, to humble our pride and challenge our foresight.

It is important to think not only of flowers. Boxwood (*Buxus sempervirens*) wears its loveliest shade of green through June. The fresh, young foliage is matte—a light, soft hue with a hint of olive, and a bit woolly-looking—all of which is highly complementary to the other plants growing around it. (A timely reminder: These days, in many regions box needs regular health inspections for pest or disease and suitable treatment if necessary.) In today's cottage-inspired gardens you will often see mounds or simple topiaries of box, planted as plain, structural anchors, around which the herbaceous plants can come and go. In early summer,

← A different kind of box parterre, with cottage garden plants threaded in among the domes of greenery. Flowers include alliums, *Gillenia trifoliata*, and roses.

→→ Jewel-rich vibrance for the start of summer, from *Gladiolus byzantinus*, ruby red peony 'Buckeye Belle', foxgloves, irises, *Stipa* grasses, and amethyst *Allium hollandicum* 'Purple Sensation'.

↓ Under dappled shade, fresh lemon-and-lime foliage of *Hosta* 'Spritzer'. Growing hostas in large pots lifts them away from the ground, helping make them less accessible to marauding slugs and snails, while other deterrents can be deployed at ground level.

for example, box sits well with foxgloves, shrub roses, and herbaceous peonies. Or perhaps accompanied by bulbs, such as alliums, or the striking magenta *Gladiolus communis* subsp. *byzantinus*, often seen in olive groves and neglected pastures in its homeland of the Mediterranean region.

Still with foliage, I feel that hostas are at their loveliest in early June, before the flowers emerge and dilute the crisp purity of their luscious leaves. Unfortunately, slugs and snails also think hostas are mightily luscious. Where these mollusks are a problem, if grown at all, more success is likely for hostas in pots, which can be easily monitored and just "dropped in" (Gertrude Jekyll's term) among other plants to enhance a display for a brief period—preferably during a dry spell when the pests have gone into hiding.

The green, felty leaves of culinary sage romp away with fresh growth in June and, for contrast, we have eruptions of bronze-leaved fennel *Foeniculum vulgare* 'Purpureum' popping up here and there among them. It should be admitted, though, the fennel chose this combination of its own accord, as it tends to do. Fennel self-sows everywhere and can be attractive temporary company among

↑ A startling scarlet poppy unfurls among fragrant, edible fronds of bronze fennel, *Foeniculum vulgare* 'Purpureum'.

short-lived seasonal plants, with some surprisingly pretty effects from its filigree foliage alone. In a patch of gravel, it has muscled in among other self-sowers in quite a pretty arrangement, where fennel's fresh ferny fronds are joined by green alkanet (which actually has royal blue, forget-me-not flowers) and emerging self-sown poppies. All of them are enjoyed by pollinators, with the alkanet and poppies especially liked by bumblebees; further into summer, when the fennel pushes out its umbels of flowers, it is a magnet for hoverflies.

The Cedric Morris Irises

FREQUENTLY IT HAS BEEN KEEN AMATEUR GARDENERS WHO HAVE painstakingly bred superior cultivars of their chosen flower. One of them is the artist Cedric Morris (1899–1982), who decided to breed (and ultimately, paint) a range of old-fashioned irises in the 'Tall Bearded' category, at his Suffolk garden, Benton End. Morris bred the irises, in his own words, for "form, poise, color, texture and general design." What could be a more worthwhile horticultural undertaking? Irises are fascinating in their mutable colors, and the 'Tall Bearded' kind seem to bloom just around the moment when spring is departing but proper summer has not yet commenced.

← An artist's palette: Some Cedric Morris irises at Hemingford Grey, Cambridgeshire. They include 'Benton Opal', 'Benton Nutkin', 'Benton Deidre', 'Benton Lorna', and velvety purple 'Storrington'.

From the many thousands of seedling irises raised by Morris, spanning from the mid-1930s to 1960s, some ninety of them were selected and named by him, many of them carrying the 'Benton' prefix—with the best of the best also named after those close to him, members of his family, his friends, and his cats. By now, many are lost to cultivation, but horticulturist Sarah Cook, a former long-serving head gardener at Sissinghurst Castle in Kent, made it her retirement project in 2004 to locate and bring together as many of the surviving Morris cultivars as she could find. Two decades on, she now holds the National Collection, which amounts to about one-third of the original ninety, and has organized their propagation for the nursery trade to ensure their survival.

The Morris irises have a delicacy in their quivering petals and subtle watercolor tints that make them especially appealing for a traditional cottage garden ambience. Their character is different from that of modern commercial iris breeders, such as Cayeux in France, and Schreiner's in Oregon in the United States, which may be looking for repeat flowering, frilly blooms, strong colorways, and thick petals for weather resistance, among other also worthwhile qualities.

While tall, bearded irises are not difficult to grow, they do have some particular requirements in order to thrive. Plant them in fertile but always free-draining, loamy soil in a sunny location, sheltered from strong, destabilizing winds, which can rock their shallow root systems. The rhizomes, which visually resemble fresh gingerroots, need to be close to and visible on the soil surface and facing the sun so they get a good summer baking (at least six to eight hours of direct sunshine is a requirement). Their preference is for neutral pH to slightly alkaline, so a light annual dressing of garden lime or powdered dolomite after flowering may be helpful to raise the pH in some instances. A general feed of balanced fertilizer (equal parts of nitrogen, phosphorous, and potassium) applied in early spring and again about a month after flowering is over, will be helpful.

Good companion plants include more of the same! Irises are very effective planted en masse. Alternatively, *Allium cristophii*, love-in-a-mist (*Nigella damascena*), *Centranthus ruber*, or annual poppies are complementary flowers that will not crowd out and shade the sunbathing iris rhizomes.

Iris Lore, Colors, and Beards

→ Among the multitude of irises raised by Morris, he looked for "form, poise, color, texture and general design," naming the best and discarding the rest. Some of the chosen include:

CLOCKWISE FROM TOP RIGHT
— Silvery 'Benton Argent'
— Caramel 'Benton Susan'
— Rosy 'Benton Arundel'
— Pale 'Benton Primrose'
— Ethereal 'Benton Olive'
— Two-tone 'Benton Lorna'

When one thinks of typical cottage garden irises, they are usually of the "bearded" type, known as *Iris × germanica*, believed to have been a naturally occurring hybrid between two other wild European species. Quite where and when they met, a long time ago, does not appear to have been confirmed. Nevertheless, *Iris × germanica* (also know widely as just *Iris germanica*, without the hybrid "x" confirmation) is quite widespread in Europe and there are many thousands of named cultivars, covering virtually the entire color spectrum. That is only fitting, really, since the flower is named after the Greek goddess Iris, a messenger of the gods, who dressed herself in a cloak of a thousand colors and painted the sky with the arc of the rainbow.

The bearded iris is called so because of the bushy "beards" that are prominently seen on the falls (lower petals) of each flower. The beard has a useful role in attracting and guiding pollinating insects to the flower's pollen and nectar. It is a vibrant feature in its own right, often (but not always) bringing an interesting shot of yellow-orange into the center of each bloom.

Not all bearded irises are "tall." They come in six categories, according to height. The shortest are Miniature Dwarf Bearded, then Standard Dwarf Bearded, Intermediate Dwarf Bearded, Miniature Tall Bearded, Border Bearded, and finally, Tall Bearded.

The classifications are useful, because they can help gardeners choose irises appropriate to their garden space and flowering schedule. The shortest categories bloom earliest, by mid-spring, and are the best choice for windy locations; you can move up the scale according to how sheltered your garden is, or how far into the season you prefer your irises to flower. Some bearded irises have been bred to bloom again, in late summer, and are known as "rebloomers," an accurate but odd word, which sounds somewhat like a dating organization for seniors (and I suppose it is, in a way, for these lovely, ephemeral flowers).

In the Height of the Summer Months

The summer cottage garden is never static, always evolving. The nursery industry thrives on novelty and improvement, so breeding new varieties with various desirable attributes can be helpful to any gardener. Plants bred to have better pest and disease resistance, greater ability to cope with less-than-ideal weather (too hot, too cold, too wet, too dry, etc.), broader color ranges, or longer flowering periods are all helpful attributes that plant breeders have become very good at achieving.

Having said that, the old-fashioned cottage garden flowers—the simple columbines and fragrant heritage sweet peas, the original, pink-purple foxglove of woodland clearings, pansies with "funny faces," and single-flowered hollyhocks have timeless appeal.

The plantsman and celebrated garden author Christopher Lloyd (1921–2006) was very knowledgeable about both old and new plants, understanding the heritage of the old varieties but interested in experimenting with the new (when they had merit) at his well-known Great Dixter garden. Among the foxgloves, he leaned toward the original kind and noted:

> Foxgloves have the same flowering season as lupines—I mean the biennial strains of our native *Digitalis purpurea*. Sometimes we save our own seed from a good white one that is growing in isolation. We like the 'Glittering Prizes' strain, with heavily spotted glove fingers, or the all-apricot-colored strain. I see no point in dwarf foxgloves—their height is no disadvantage even in the smallest garden; nor in strains in which the flowers are arranged all round the spike, rather than on one side, as is natural. The one-sided kinds always look towards me, in my experience, and they are graceful.

The rose has been called the undisputed queen of the summer garden and, for many of us, it is. The perfect pink shades of many old roses, such as 'Ispahan' and 'Queen of Denmark', the golden-centered, deep claret rosettes of 'Tuscany Superb', or the full, deep magenta-purple blooms of 'William Lobb' bursting out of mossy-green buds, are long-awaited, to be relished in one intense June moment. Fortunately, there are also the repeat flowerers, both old and modern, that prolong the rose season and enhance the garden in various ways as summer progresses (page 107).

The start of summer is the moment to plant tender species that will invigorate the garden over a longer season, getting into their stride as the weeks progress. Pelargoniums, dahlias, heliotropes, calibrachoas, tender salvias, and so on may be put outdoors with confidence that damaging frosts are now well out of the way. Lifting some of these special plants away from the ground and into containers offers numerous advantages, giving them increased protection from pests (they are also easier to check over) and enabling a change of

planting medium from the surrounding garden topsoil, into something that will suit them better. It also makes enjoyment of their flowers—and in some cases, their fragrance—more accessible.

For example, the deliciously aromatic *Salvia greggii* varieties produce their flowers across a wide spectrum of colors. In the ground or in containers, these salvias make good companions for varieties of *Lavandula* × *intermedia*, such as 'Grosso' and 'Phenomenal', which are themselves capable of blooming over a long season. They all enjoy the same conditions: a bright, sunny location and light-textured, freely draining (but not parched) soil. As our own ground is very heavy and gets easily waterlogged in a poor summer, I grow these indispensable summer staples in large containers filled with free-draining, loamy potting mix that gives their root balls plenty of chance to expand. Provided the lavenders' spent flowers are deadheaded periodically, we (and the bees) can look forward to a deliciously fragrant and relaxed-looking display from midsummer to early autumn.

↑ A perfect summer partnership for pots: Downy-leaved *Helichrysum petiolare* 'Limelight' and a contrasting pelargonium that will flower for a long season, when regularly deadheaded.

→→ Soft tones from 'Hidcote' lavenders, white foxgloves, *Centranthus ruber* 'Alba', rose 'Penelope', and catmint *Nepeta racemosa* 'Walker's Low'.

COTTAGE PLANTS FOR SUMMER

Annals and Biennials

- *Alcea rosea*, hollyhock
- *Ammi majus*, false Queen Anne's lace
- *Calendula officinalis*, common marigold
- *Calibrachoa* × *hybrida*, million bells
- *Campanula medium*, Canterbury bells
- *Clarkia amoena*, godetia, satin flower
- *Cleome hassleriana*, spider flower
- *Cosmos bipinnatus*, cosmos
- *Dianthus barbatus*, sweet William
- *Digitalis purpurea*, foxglove
- *Eschscholzia californica*, California poppy
- *Helianthus annuus*, sunflower
- *Hesperis matronalis*, sweet rocket
- *Lathyrus odoratus*, sweet pea
- *Matthiola longipetala*, night-scented stock
- *Nicotiana alata*, sweet tobacco
- *Nigella damascena*, love-in-a-mist
- *Oenothera biennis*, evening primrose
- *Papaver* 'Mother of Pearl', pastel poppy
- *Petunia* × *atkinsiana*, hybrid petunia
- *Tagetes patula*, French marigold
- *Tropaeolum majus*, garden nasturtium
- *Zinnia elegans*, zinnia

COTTAGE PLANTS FOR SUMMER

Perennials and Bulbs

- *Achillea millefolium*, yarrow
- *Agastache foeniculum*, anise hyssop
- *Alchemilla mollis*, lady's mantle
- *Allium* 'Globemaster', purple allium (bulb)
- *Aquilegia vulgaris*, columbine, granny's bonnet
- *Asclepias tuberosa*, butterfly weed
- *Centranthus ruber*, red valerian, Jupiter's beard
- *Delphinium elatum*, perennial delphinium
- *Erigeron karvinskianus*, Mexican fleabane, Santa Barbara daisy
- *Eryngium planum*, sea holly
- *Gaura lindheimeri*, beeblossom
- *Geranium* spp., (various) hardy geranium
- *Gladiolus communis* subsp. *byzantinus*, wild gladiolus
- *Hemerocallis* hybrids, daylily
- *Iris* × *germanica*, bearded iris
- *Leucanthemum* × *superbum*, shasta daisy
- *Lilium* spp., (many), lily (bulb)
- *Lupinus* hybrids, lupin, lupine
- *Monarda didyma*, bee balm
- *Nepeta* × *faassenii*, catmint
- *Paeonia lactiflora*, herbaceous peony
- *Penstemon digitalis*, beardtongue
- *Phlox paniculata*, garden phlox
- *Rudbeckia* spp., black-eyed susan
- *Salvia nemorosa*, Balkan sage
- *Stachys byzantina*, lamb's ears
- *Verbena bonariensis*, purple top
- *Veronicastrum virginicum*, Culver's root
- *Viola tricolor* var. *hortensis* pansy

Scent in the Summer Garden

The world is full of smells; many we can easily detect, others we cannot. Some smells are welcome and enjoyable; others produce reactions of loathing or disgust. The alluring aroma of a bakery or coffee shop may stimulate feelings of comfort or whet the appetite, while certain floral scents might conjure memories of people or places in our past or simply uplift one's mood.

In the animal kingdom, a sense of smell is often linked to finding potential food sources. For example, turkey vultures soaring way up in the sky on thermals rely heavily on their keen olfactory senses, detecting whiffs of carrion from more than a mile away, even if it is concealed in a forest. On the other hand (and this is irksome for the grower), slugs can smell ripe strawberries some two hundred yards (180 meters) away, using retractable sensory tentacles on their heads. Indeed, their sense of smell is so finely developed they can detect, at a distance, the volatile organic compounds released by young hosta leaves—premium caviar to slugs and snails—again, to the exasperation of gardeners.

Fortunately, planting the garden for summer fragrances that we enjoy sometimes confounds the predations of mollusks, which are not at all attracted to lavender, rosemary, *Calamintha*, and other aromatic members of the mint family, *Lamiaceae*. (Nevertheless, if pressed, they might hide under them! Check regularly for these slithery squatters.) Recently, I discovered by accident that it might be possible to grow hostas successfully after all, even in inclement England, by putting them on the terrace among aromatic herbs, which seem to mask the hostas' fugitive fragrances. (For more on herbs, see p. 235.)

It makes sense to put your prized scented flowers (and foliage) somewhere that will benefit from their moment of glory—near an open window or doorway, for example, or, especially, somewhere sheltered that can be made into a pleasant sitting area. A windy spot is no good at all, since any scent is quickly blown away; but a sheltered terrace beside a sun-baked house wall that releases warmth through the late afternoon and evening is ideal, encouraging plants to reveal their scents.

← Time for tea: At Stevington, Bedfordshire, a sheltered sitting area is just the right place to grow a fragrant climbing rose such as 'Cecile Brunner'.

→→ Perfumed partners for a wall, trellis, arbor, or pergola: The honeysuckle *Lonicera periclymenum* 'Graham Thomas' and richly scented climbing rose 'Alchymist'.

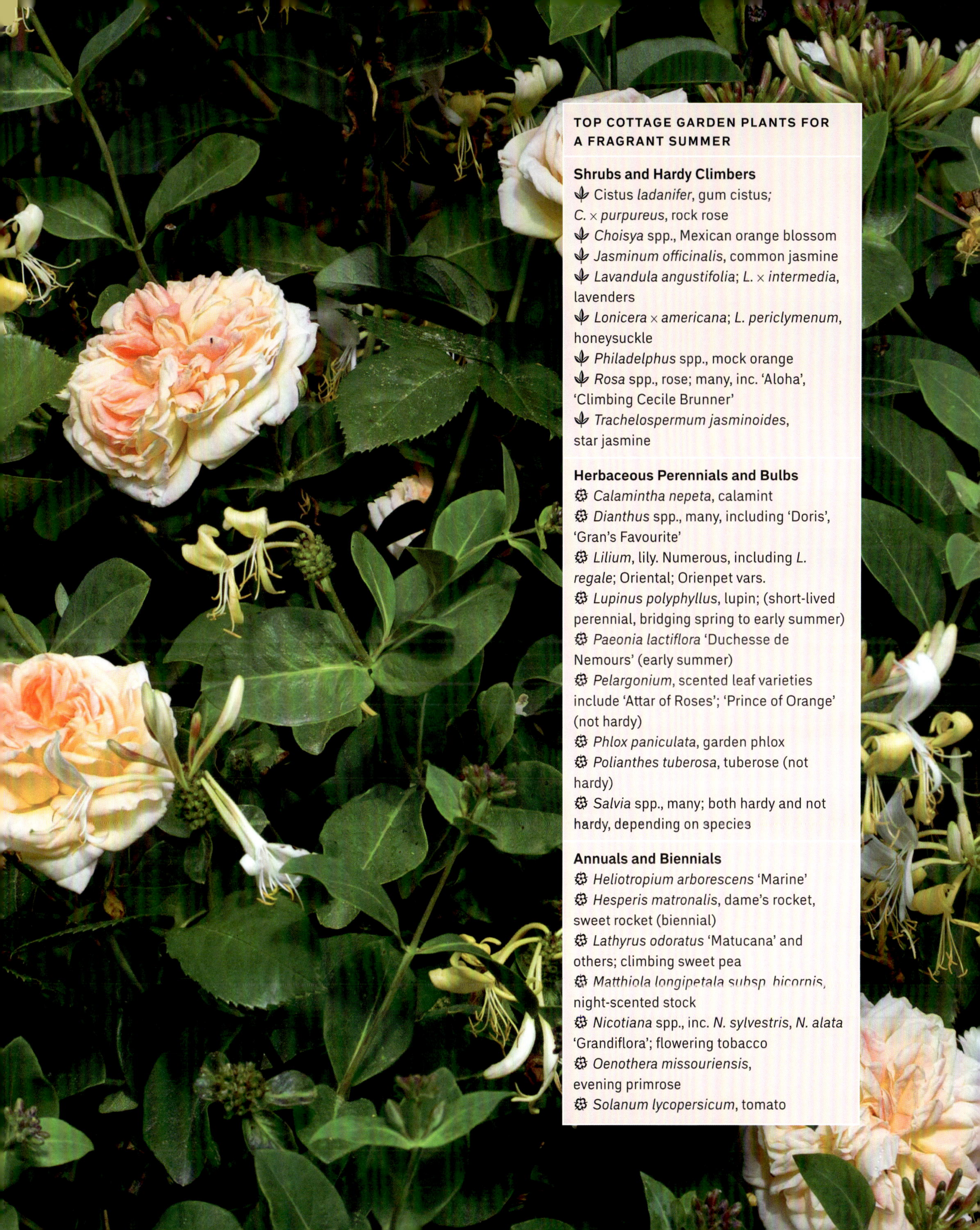

TOP COTTAGE GARDEN PLANTS FOR A FRAGRANT SUMMER

Shrubs and Hardy Climbers

- Cistus *ladanifer*, gum cistus; *C.* × *purpureus*, rock rose
- *Choisya* spp., Mexican orange blossom
- *Jasminum officinalis*, common jasmine
- *Lavandula angustifolia*; *L.* × *intermedia*, lavenders
- *Lonicera* × *americana*; *L. periclymenum*, honeysuckle
- *Philadelphus* spp., mock orange
- *Rosa* spp., rose; many, inc. 'Aloha', 'Climbing Cecile Brunner'
- *Trachelospermum jasminoides*, star jasmine

Herbaceous Perennials and Bulbs

- *Calamintha nepeta*, calamint
- *Dianthus* spp., many, including 'Doris', 'Gran's Favourite'
- *Lilium*, lily. Numerous, including *L. regale*; Oriental; Orienpet vars.
- *Lupinus polyphyllus*, lupin; (short-lived perennial, bridging spring to early summer)
- *Paeonia lactiflora* 'Duchesse de Nemours' (early summer)
- *Pelargonium*, scented leaf varieties include 'Attar of Roses'; 'Prince of Orange' (not hardy)
- *Phlox paniculata*, garden phlox
- *Polianthes tuberosa*, tuberose (not hardy)
- *Salvia* spp., many; both hardy and not hardy, depending on species

Annuals and Biennials

- *Heliotropium arborescens* 'Marine'
- *Hesperis matronalis*, dame's rocket, sweet rocket (biennial)
- *Lathyrus odoratus* 'Matucana' and others; climbing sweet pea
- *Matthiola longipetala* subsp. *bicornis*, night-scented stock
- *Nicotiana* spp., inc. *N. sylvestris*, *N. alata* 'Grandiflora'; flowering tobacco
- *Oenothera missouriensis*, evening primrose
- *Solanum lycopersicum*, tomato

Another option could be a purpose-built gazebo, where fragrant climbers can trail over and waft their perfume around the interior. Roses, jasmines, and honeysuckles are ideal for this treatment; a rose with good scent over a prolonged season, such as luscious, deep pink 'Aloha' or the delicate pink 'Climbing Cecile Brunner' can hardly be bettered.

"Every garden should have at least one *Jasminum officinale*," advised Margery Fish, "for there is nothing so ravishing as the scent of the common jasmine. One of my earliest recollections is being taken down the garden path at a seaside cottage to a little house romantically wreathed in jasmine. I believe that jasmine was the popular treatment for such places, and quite rightly." As someone who practiced what she preached, Fish created a summerhouse out of an existing garden building and engulfed it with jasmine, preserving the childhood memory.

→ A gallery of dependably fragrant flowers with old-fashioned cottage garden charm:

TOP ROW
— Dame's violet *Hesperis matronalis*
— Pastel-flowered *Salvia microphylla*
— *Trachelospermum jasminoides*

MIDDLE ROW
— Rose-scented geranium *Pelargonium graveolens*
— Regal lily *Lilium regale*
— *Calamintha nepeta* 'Blue Cloud'

BOTTOM ROW
— *Jasminum officinale* 'Clotted Cream'
— *Lavandula* x *intermedia* 'Grosso'
— Fragrant old rose 'Ispahan'

Scent preferences are quite personal and can change over the course of a lifetime. For years I disliked both lavender and pungent tomato leaves, but now regard them both with delight, as two of the essential scents of summer. Some people cannot abide the volatile oils in the foliage of clary sage, *Salvia sclarea* var. *turkestanica*, an ancient, medicinal plant and cottage garden herb. Stephen Lacey, author of *Scent in Your Garden* (1991), describes it as one of the "few really nasty odors . . . a nasty, sweaty aroma." Slugs do not like it either, but to my nose, clary sage smells pleasantly spicy-citrus and very reminiscent of grapefruit.

Floral fragrance is usually very helpful to pollinators, which, like the vultures and slugs, pick up scent trails to source their sustenance. Often, it is white, or very pale flowers, that release the strongest scents, just as evening approaches. Being pollinated by nocturnal creatures such as moths, they have no need for bright colors to advertise themselves, but they are great perfume factories, with increased visibility in moonlight. Jasmines, tuberoses, evening primroses, night-scented stocks, and tobacco flowers fall into this category, and it is pleasant to have some of these flowers around when relaxing outdoors at sundown.

"Perfumers and flavorists [flavor chemists] are constantly humbled by the greatest perfumer of them all, Nature," declared scent expert Luca Turin. "A walk through a rose garden in June will reveal every varietal to have a unique smell, ranging from that peculiarly lemony style which one never encounters in perfume, to the heavy oriental via all shades of peppery tea. A ripe mango, with its combination of incense-like austerity and sulphurous decadence, is a perfumery idea of pure genius." Mango trees are not an option for those of us in northern climes, but peppery tea, oriental perfumes, resinous incense, and much else besides will be found among the plants within these pages.

Color Themes for Summer

Once, long ago, before the age of satellite navigation and personal cell phones, I was due to visit an exceptional gardener, to write a magazine feature about his cottage garden. I was lost and needed to ask directions from someone local. My showing the address to a passerby was not enlightening, but when I explained my mission, he exclaimed, "Oh, you're looking for *the beautiful garden*" (as local people called it), and then he was able to direct me precisely.

The cottage was set well back from the road, half hidden by a profusion of flowers. A perfect green lawn rolled out in front of it, nearly to the road, but deep borders all around the perimeter were packed with a riot of colorful summer flowers. Marigolds, petunias, nasturtiums, foxgloves, begonias, busy lizzies, and much else besides were all clashing and thriving, with marvelous, excitable energy; their creator had a correspondingly sunny personality. It was not the sort of "tasteful," color-themed approach that Gertrude Jekyll spent years experimenting with and conveying to her readers, but she would doubtless have enjoyed the cottage garden's exuberance, its creator's horticultural skills, and the lack of any pretension.

Color matches (and color clashes) tend to be personal creative expressions, but people have investigated and theorized for centuries the origins and "meanings" of colors, their effects on mood, and a color's own relationship to others on the "color wheel." Such considerations probably go back to ancient times. When Isaac Newton presented his *New Theory about Light and Colours* to the Royal Society in 1672, he described how his experiments indicated that a beam of sunlight passing through a prism formed a band of colors like a rainbow, ergo, sunlight is composed of a mixture of differently colored rays. Later, he presented his conclusions in a circular color wheel diagram, showing the first graphic representation of color saturation.

Goethe's Color Wheel of 1809 arranged colors in what he called their natural order, but he also included aesthetic qualities under the title of "allegorical, symbolic, mystic use of color." His theories strongly affected the painter J. M. W. Turner, among others. As an art student at London's Central School of Art and Design from 1861, and under the influence of John Ruskin (then Slade Professor of Art at Oxford), the young Gertrude Jekyll carefully studied and copied Turner's art. She absorbed the flowing masses of "warm" and "cool" colors in great works such as *Burning of the Houses of Lords and Commons, 16 October, 1834*, and *The Fighting Temeraire* (1838), much later putting that learning into the

← Variations on a theme of gold: Coneflower *Echinacea paradoxa*, *Euphorbia seguieriana*, and "Spanish oats" *Stipa gigantea*.

→→ A blue-themed border with violas, linaria, eryngiums, *Salvia verticillata* 'Purple Rain', penstemons, and delphiniums at Grafton Cottage, Staffordshire.

main summer border in her garden at Munstead Wood. The two-hundred-foot-long border progressed from blue flowers and gray foliage at one end, through soft pinks and pale yellows to a crescendo of fiery red, scarlet, and orange in the middle, before receding again to blue and gray at the far end. Jekyll also understood the significance of complementary colors (those opposite each other on the color wheel), citing examples in her planting plans.

A great shortage of garden staff occurred during and after the First World War; finances and staff were further reduced by the Second World War, making high-maintenance flower schemes fall out of fashion for decades. Borders were grassed over or replanted with low-maintenance shrubs. Undemanding ground-covering plants became popular.

→ A symphony of summer pinks with *Dahlia* 'Peter', *Phlox paniculata* 'Laura', *Achillea millefolium* 'Fire King', *Persicaria* 'Firetail', and *Lobelia* 'Hadspen Purple'.

→→ When opposites attract: Complementary shades on the color wheel, with red-hot pokers *Kniphofia* 'Tawny King' and 'Amsterdam' and *Agapanthus* 'Gem'.

Floral interest returned, however, with a Jekyll and Arts and Crafts gardens revival, from the beginning of the 1980s to the end of the century. In this period, with a greater than ever before range of plant material available and plenty of full-color publications to guide the way, old-fashioned flowers, "color" gardening, and cottage gardening became fashionable again. Revised, color-illustrated editions of Jekyll's most famous books were published, and many new ones concerned with Jekyll's interests came to the market. Among them were *Colour in Your Garden* by Penelope Hobhouse (1985); *V. Sackville-West: The Illustrated Garden Book* (1986); *Old Garden Flowers* by Brian Halliwell (1987); *The Victorian Flower Garden* by Jennifer Davies (1991); *The Cottage Gardener's Companion* by Clive Lane (1993); *Geoff Hamilton's Cottage Gardens* (1995); *The Gardener's Book of Colour* by Andrew Lawson (1996); *Colour by Design* by Nori and Sandra Pope (1998); *The Gardens of William Morris* by Hamilton, Hart, and Simmons (1998); and *Colour for Adventurous Gardeners* by Christopher Lloyd (2001).

As Hugh Johnson has wryly observed,

> The short cut to making a big impact with color, as with everything else in the garden, is to be ruthlessly single-minded. If you can bring yourself to devote a part of your garden to one color only, with variety limited to heights, shapes and tones, you will have a picture people will take away with them. . . . Strong doses of one color undeniably affect the mood of the viewer. If yellow is warming and cheering, soft blues and mauves are soothing, red and orange are exciting, white is at once peaceful and lively, fresh and yet somehow formal. White is much the easiest single color to handle. The choice of white flowers is almost infinite. . . Gently creamy-white flowers also help to keep the mood calm, where laundry whiteness all around might prove dazzling and irritating. In any color scheme the leaves have a part to play at least as great as the flowers.

Pages 100–01 and 103 illustrate two examples of single-color themes in a traditional cottage garden, and pages 104–105 a fine example of saturated complementary colors at the height of summer.

7 · A Rose Is a Rose Is a Rose . . .

> The history of the rose is intimately interwoven with the movements of civilization, the march of armies, and the gradual knitting together by mutual needs of the countries of the world. The rose, as we know it today, has drawn its ancestors from Persia and Armenia, from Syria and China, and as these countries have gradually come in touch with European civilization so has the rose, little by little, assumed the form and colors which make it today the most popular of garden flowers.
>
> — EDWARD BUNYARD, 1936

THEY MAY HAVE THEIR ORIGINS IN MUCH OLDER AND WARMER PARTS of the world but in the collective imagination, roses seem almost to have been made to adorn country cottages and their gardens. The image of a pretty home with roses pinned to the walls and around the windows is charming and enduring. Indeed, a number of attractive villages in England's Cotswolds area (comprising parts of Gloucestershire and Oxfordshire) receive busloads of visitors from the farthest reaches of the world every summer; they want to see and enjoy, firsthand, the quaint vernacular homes garlanded with roses and guarded by platoons of hollyhocks.

Apart from all their virtues of scent, color, cultural history, and versatility, roses are popular because most of them are incredibly easy to grow. Plant them well, with attention to their needs at the start and they will give many years of pleasure in due season. They tend to be hungry plants, liking a feed and a soil-enriching mulch of old manure every year and some perform best from a pruning routine, but a healthy rose will carry on just "being a rose" without too much fuss or anxiety expended on our part. As with other plants, success with roses comes from choosing the right one for the right location.

Generally, roses thrive in sunny locations with some six to eight hours of direct sunlight required daily for best results in growth and flowering. Some will also give a good account of themselves in partial shade, although flowering may well be less abundant. In the dappled shade of small trees, I have had success with 'Harlow Carr', a tough and thorny little rose producing masses of fragrant pink flowers of old-fashioned character; also with the indestructible *Rosa rugosa*

← The attractive brick wall of an old cottage, further enhanced by the repeat-flowering, thornless rose 'Zephirine Drouhin' and the fragrant rose 'Ispahan', joined by the perennial wallflower, *Erysimum* 'Bowles Mauve'.

→→ A trellis framework supports the fluttering, cerise petals of *Rosa* x *odorata* 'Mutabilis', while an arch over the doorway is resplendent with climbing rose 'Ghislaine de Feligonde'.

'Alba' (pure white) and the wonderful 'white rose of York' *Rosa* × *alba* 'Alba Semi-plena', an ancient and robust rose. The last two are adored by bumblebees when in bloom and they produce rosehips afterward, much enjoyed by the blackbirds and pigeons.

When selecting any particular rose, consider what it is expected to do. If it is being planted near a window or doorway that is regularly opened, or near to somewhere you like to sit, think about the best perfumed varieties. Likewise, the pleasure of walking through a rose arch or pergola is magnified if the blooms on your climbing plants are perfumed as well as pretty. In this respect, the deep pink climber 'Zephirine Drouhin', a fragrant mid-eighteenth-century rose, can be a great choice for walk-through structures in the garden, flowering over a long period, and it is also thornless. The China rose 'Mutabilis', also known as the Butterfly Rose, is nice for a wall or trellis and sends out wiry stems with fluttery flowers across a very long season. Its name refers to the petals' remarkable color changes, from soft yellow through pink, to crimson as they age. 'Mutabilis' has a very natural look and fits in well with contemporary "wilder" plantings in the garden. I have one growing beside *Drimys lanceolata* (syn. *Tasmannia lanceolata*) in a relaxed part of the garden, where the rose weaves into the evergreen *Drimys* here and there, blending with the dark green shrub's crimson stems. See the table in this chapter for some more great choices of roses for different situations.

← Fellowship of the rose: Nine beautiful varieties that have withstood the test of time (left to right):

TOP ROW
— 'Cardinal de Richelieu'
— 'Variegata di Bologna'
— 'Ispahan'

MIDDLE ROW
— 'Adélaide d'Orléans'
— 'Buff Beauty'
— 'Madame Hardy'

BOTTOM ROW
— 'Graham Thomas'
— 'Nevada'
— 'Grace'

← Supremely prickly, the wingthorn rose, best grown where the sunlight can get behind it. *Rosa sericea* subsp. *omeiensis* f. *pteracantha* also produces attractively simple, white-petaled flowers.

→→ A rose tunnel of spectacular blooms, including (front to back): *Rosa* 'Golden Showers', 'Dee Dee Bridgewater', 'Clair Matin', 'Pierre de Ronsard'.

8 ROSES FOR SCENT

Fragrant Cloud
Hybrid tea rose, generously flowering over a long season with spicy/fruity/citrus notes in its powerful fragrance. Coral red blooms, good for cutting, good disease resistance.

Gertrude Jekyll
Highly successful David Austin rose, named after the great gardener, herself a rose connoisseur. Large, multi-petaled "rose pink'" classic blooms with powerful Old Rose fragrance.

Great Maiden's Blush
A very old, special rose, deeply fragrant with packed and crumpled shell pink petals, lighter at the edges. Multiple buds on each stem; the once-flowering period is around midsummer.

Ispahan
Deliciously fragrant and blooming over a long season. The red buds open out into rich pink flowers, numerous per stem. A generous and healthy rose, known in the West for some two hundred years.

Madame Isaac Pereire
Deep pink-magenta flowers, very large and with a powerful fragrance. Repeat flowering in flushes from midsummer to early autumn. Suits training over an obelisk.

Margaret Merril
A multiple medal-winning, very popular floribunda rose. Repeat flowering, good for cutting, with a delicious spicy-citrus fragrance.

Paul Shirvill
Well-shaped rose of mutable apricot to shades of peach-pink. Award winning for its powerful scent, it makes a great cut flower rose.

Alba Semi-plena
Remarkable, strong, and ancient rose, said to be the medieval 'White Rose of York.' Multiple open, well-scented flowers in a single flush around midsummer, liked by bees for the visible stamens.

8 ROSES FOR REPEAT FLOWERING

Alister Stella Gray
Also known as Golden Rambler, a most attractive climber with repeat flowering. Blooms start yellow, fading to cream held in small sprays. Delicious tea rose scent.

Ballerina
A little poppet, full of charm, blooming through the season. Small, single flowers of soft pink with a central white eye, with many per stem.

Blanc Double de Coubert
Semi-double, pure white flowers, very fragrant and repeating, followed by tomato-like hips. A superb *rugosa* rose with thorny stems and healthy foliage.

Bonica
One of the most popular of all modern shrub roses, being well-behaved, fragrant, and repeat flowering in pretty soft pink.

Graham Thomas
Named after the great gardener and rosarian, a superb golden-yellow English rose. Its full and fragrant flowers are generously produced. Can potentially be grown as a climber if planted against a wall or other support.

Munstead Wood
Sultry and velvety crimson flowers like Burgundy wine, in abundance, with a light, fruity scent. Dramatic and neat; fits well into small gardens.

Mutabilis
Flowers like butterflies, lightweight and held aloft on wiry stems. Blooms continuously for many months, petals changing from yellow to pink then crimson. Best given support.

Sally Holmes
Wide spreading, can be grown on a warm and sunny wall or freestanding; showy bunches of large, single flowers opening pearly apricot-pink fading to white. Performs best in warm locations.

8 ROSES FOR PERGOLAS & ARCHES

Alberic Barbier
An old rambler with tremendous vim and vigor, easily covering a pergola or arbor in abundant blooms, yellow in bud, turning cream as they age.

Albertine
Plentiful coral-salmon buds open out to large, frilly, and characterful flowers on this captivating rambler flowering only around midsummer.

Baltimore Belle
An old American rose of the 1840s. Abundant crimson buds open to exquisite full flowers of pale pink fading to ivory on strong and graceful plants. Blooms a month later than midsummer ramblers.

Mme Gregoire Staechelin
Does its thing in one generous blooming at midsummer but worth the wait until next time. Gloriously loose and blousy large flowers of mutable pink tones; fragrant, perfect for arches.

Maigold
A healthy, hardy, and thorny-stemmed early season climber. Numerous big, golden blooms on strong canes, possibly with some extra flowers later. Eye-catching and fragrant.

Phyllis Bide
Pretty, pink, and peachy rambler ideal to train over an arbor, an arch, or a doorway. Clusters of small, characterful flowers, scented and repeating over the season.

Tess of the d'Urbervilles
Potentially an easily managed, compact climber, if grown against support such as a pillar, wall, or trellis. Sumptuous, dark crimson blooms of old rose shape, with scent.

The Pilgrim
Pale to medium yellow flowers, full petaled and abundant with spicy scent. Grown as a climber, great for arches and pergolas.

8 ROSES FOR SMALL GARDENS

Abraham Darby
Pastel tints of yellow, apricot, and pink infuse the big, full flowers, darker in the center. Fruity fragrance. A stunning, show-off plant good for allowing to tumble over a strong picket fence.

Comte de Chambord
A classic, strong and abundant mid-nineteenth-century rose with full, mid-pink flowers and heady, true rose fragrance; repeat flowering.

Fritz Nobis
Free-flowering pink with a hint of salmon, charming shrub rose, strongly scented and producing orange hips later. In a small garden it is a nice subject for training to a trellis or obelisk.

Jacqueline du Pre
A most elegant, fragrant rose bearing lots of wide open creamy-white flowers with contrasting red and gold stamens giving it a warm central glow; loved by pollinators, especially bees.

Little White Pet
A great little rose for front of border or patio containers. Clusters of small, pompom-like white flowers emerge in quantity from crimson buds. Deadheading faded flowers keeps it going for months.

Nathalie Nypels
Very pretty, pink-washed-with-cream semi-double flowers over a long season, with pleasing fragrance.

Rambling Rosie
Eye-catching clusters of small, bright red, cheerful blooms; repeat flowering across the season. A great rose for a trellis, an arch, or trained around an obelisk.

The Generous Gardener
The climbing version of this English rose is lovely on arches, trellis, or framing a doorway. Pretty, pale pink flowers with spicy scent for many months.

←← A rose by any other name: The multi-monikered 'Cyclamen Eden Rose', also known as 'Cyclamen Pierre de Ronsard' and 'Pretty in Pink Eden Climber', bred by Meilland.

→ Garden visits always provide further inspiration. Cottage garden perennials mix with abundant roses at Parc Thermal de Mondorf-les-Bainss, Luxembourg. The roses include clouds of pink 'Maid Marion' (foreground) and white-flowered 'Rambling Rector' on the tunnel.

Vita's White Garden

> There is an underplanting of various artemisias, including the old aromatic Southernwood; the silvery Cineraria maritima; the grey santolina or Cotton Lavender; and the creeping Achillea ageratifolia. Dozens of the white regale lily (grown from seed) come up through these. There are white delphiniums of the Pacific strain; white eremurus; white foxgloves in a shady place on the north side of a wall; the foam of gypsophila; the white shrubby Hydrangea grandiflora; white cistus, white tree peonies, Buddleja nivea; white campanulas and the white form of Platycodon mariesii, the Chinese bell flower. There is a group of the giant Arabian thistle, pure silver, 8ft high. . . .
>
> —VITA SACKVILLE-WEST, JULY 1955

Sissinghurst Castle, now in the care of the National Trust and known worldwide for the cottage-inspired planting in its themed gardens, is an ancient place. Long ago, it was a Saxon pig farm that would have been known as "Saxenhurst." (The old term *hurst*, meaning woodland, crops up everywhere in that formerly densely forested part of England.) Later it became an extended Tudor manor house with outbuildings, courtyards, and a fine tower. In the mid-eighteenth century it was a prison for some three thousand French sailors, held there under terrible conditions in the time of the Seven Years' War. In the nineteenth century it became lodgings for the poor, who worked its farms.

The writer Vita Sackville-West and her diplomat husband, Harold Nicolson, acquired the property in 1930, by which time it was semi-derelict and the grounds full of assorted rubbish; but it had potential for anyone with romantic ambitions and deep pockets. With much work and focus, they made it famous for its Arts and Crafts–style gardens divided into rooms separated by walls and evergreen hedges, with luxuriant, carefully planned cottage garden planting filling out its generous beds. Owing to the nature of the old property, consisting of several individual buildings and cottages, they used different buildings for different pastimes, depending upon the time of day.

Among its themed areas is the White Garden, a triumph in the genre of monochromatic planting, using a mixture of white- and off-white roses, shrubs,

← A magnificent jar and iron arbor bearing cascades of *Rosa mulliganii* create the focal point in the heart of the White Garden at Sissinghurst. Cottage garden flowers around it include *Lilium regale* 'Album', *Hydrangea quercifolia*, white foxgloves, and violas.

↑ Another view across the White Garden, later in the season. Within the box-hedged beds are paddle-leaved woodland tobacco, *Nicotiana sylvestris*; white-flowered cosmos; silvery *Artemisia ludoviciana*; and downy lamb's ears, *Stachys byzantine.*

perennials, and annuals that carry a changing vision of flowering beauty from spring to autumn, although at its zenith in summer. Sackville-West announced it with diffidence in her weekly gardening column for *The Observer* newspaper in January 1950:

> For my own part, I am trying to make a grey, green, and white garden. This is an experiment which I ardently hope may be successful, though I doubt it. One's best ideas seldom play up in practice to one's expectations, especially in gardening, where everything looks so well on paper and in the catalogues, but fails so lamentably in fulfilment after you have tucked your plans into the soil. Still, one hopes. . . . I don't want to boast in advance about my grey, green and white garden. It may be a terrible failure.

Sissinghurst's White Garden is not the world's first, but it is the best known, partly due to Sackville-West's *Observer* column and other writings; paying visitors were also able to explore it. Earlier white gardens had been made by the American plantsman Lawrence Johnston, at Hidcote Manor, Gloucestershire, and by his friend, the American novelist Edith Wharton, in the early twentieth century. Perhaps they were both influenced by Gertrude Jekyll at Munstead Wood (p. 141), whose experiments in color theory had been going on for many years before she published *Colour in the Flower Garden* (1908, later republished as *Colour Schemes for the Flower Garden*).

In August 1917 Sackville-West and her mother, Lady Sackville, joined Edwin Lutyens on a visit to Gertrude Jekyll at Munstead Wood, where they saw Jekyll's tonal borders at firsthand, including her "Grey Garden" of silver foliage plants and white flowers, with the whites set off by hints of pale pastel blooms here and there. At the time, Sackville-West was planning a yellow-and-white area for the garden she and her husband were making at Long Barn, their earlier home not far from Sissinghurst.

It was not recorded as a very jolly event. Sackville-West noted, "Miss Jekyll rather fat, and rather grumbly; garden not at its best, but can see it must be lovely." To modern eyes, her comment seems starkly devoid of empathy, since their visit was at the height of the Third Battle of Ypres (Passchendaele), one of the most intense of battles in the First World War, with its constant bombardments and heavy casulaties, blasting away only some sixty miles away from the Kent coast. At the time, gardens everywhere were short-staffed, including at Munstead Wood, the men having been mobilized for the war effort.

Biographer Jane Brown has pointed out a key feature of Sissinghurst's White Garden for the Nicolson family at the time. "Nothing more nor less than Vita's being a 'night owl' seems to have been responsible for her first idea about masses of white flowers. Her days were not only too well occupied to spare much time, she actually preferred to walk abroad in the dusk and darkness. . . . It must also be remembered that the occupants of Sissinghurst Castle saw far more of their garden at night than most garden owners do . . . they had to walk through it to reach their beds and any meal."

Other than the castle's special collection of old roses, white lilies are a key feature of the place in due season. In *Some Flowers*, written before the Second World War, Sackville-West first mentioned the white lilies "seen by twilight or moonlight gleaming under the shadow of a thick wood." The wild white ox-eye daisies, appropriately also known as moon daisies (*Leucanthemum vulgare*) are a feature of English roadsides and meadows in May and June, luminescent in their thousands at dusk. They enchanted her during crepuscular walks into the countryside with a pet Alsatian at her heels and probably helped foster ideas for the white garden that continues to enchant and inspire the property's visitors to this day.

→→ Pastel tints for midsummer, including hollyhocks, delphiniums, *Alcea rosea*, *Campanula persicifolia* 'Alba', *Echium* 'Blue Bedder', centaurea, pansies, blue and pink cornflowers. Grafton Cottage, Staffordshire.

8 · Hydrangeas

VERSATILE HYDRANGEAS HAVE BEEN CHERISHED COTTAGE GARDEN plants since the eighteenth century, when traders and collectors started to acquire these new, showy plants. In 1736, at just about the same moment he was sending bulbs of tuberoses to his friend, John Custis IV of Williamsburg (p. 41), the English merchant Peter Collinson received from Virginia seeds of an unusual unclassified American plant. In 1753, Carl Linnaeus, the Swedish "father of taxonomy," named the plants *Hydrangea arborescens*, in the process founding a new genus and its first recorded species. More hydrangeas followed, some from North America and many more from East Asia, which brought a wider range of flower shapes and colors into the arena as well as more species.

While hydrangeas began as rare and "supremely magnificent" plants for the Georgian gardening elite, they are easy to grow from cuttings and therefore did not take long to be much more widely cultivated and enjoyed. In the nineteenth century, potted hydrangeas were indispensable plants for the conservatory, bringing glamour with their bold shapes and a touch of the exotic.

Most hybrid cultivars can be roughly divided into the very familiar "hortensia" (or "mophead") kinds (producing showy "blobs" of sterile flowers) and "lacecap" types, which have flattened flower heads bearing a cluster of tiny, fertile flowers in the center, surrounded by a crown of attractive, sterile florets. Especially refined and beautiful are the varieties of *Hydrangea serrata*, hailing from the mountains of Japan and Korea, bearing delicate lacecaps and bred into an alluring collection of colorways. There are also climbing hydrangeas, such as *H. petiolaris*, which can be slow to get going, but once firmly established, will clamber up considerably high walls if allowed to do so, putting out foamy cascades of creamy-white lacecaps from June onward. Some of the more traditional hortensias make popular gift plants, sold over many months in florists, supermarkets, and garden stores. These can be enjoyed indoors for a short while, then transplanted into the garden to achieve their full potential.

Many hydrangeas thrive in partial shade and can usually cope well in urban plots overshadowed for part of the day by buildings, or in the open garden among the dappled shade of taller shrubs or nearby trees. Conversely,

← Provided their nutrient and water requirements are met, hydrangeas make good specimens for large pots; in this case, a pure white hortensia or mophead type, *Hydrangea macrophylla* 'Rahic'.

→→ Cone-shaped flower heads of *Hydrangea paniculata* 'Little Lime' joined by pale pink *Hydrangea macrophylla* and white wind flower, *Anemone x hybrida* 'Honorine Jobert'.

↑ Glamorous shrubs with a touch of the exotic, hydrangeas bear their summer blooms in a broad variety of colors:

ABOVE LEFT TO RIGHT:
- *Hydrangea paniculata* 'Athena'
- A *Hydrangea aspera* hybrid
- *Hydrangea macrophylla* 'Frillibet'
- *Hydrangea serrata* 'Kurenai'
- *Hydrangea serrata* 'Blue Deckle'
- *Hydrangea macrophylla* 'Merveille Sanguine'

hydrangeas are also very familiar seaside garden plants, where they seem to appreciate the bracing and humid air, although too much sunshine may burn out the flowers rather rapidly. The charming seaside towns of New England's Cape Cod, with their traditional homes and cottages, have become especially well known for their hydrangea displays in due season, even including a hydrangea festival in July.

The one thing hydrangeas do not enjoy, wherever they are grown, is dry soil. These are thirsty and hungry plants, needing regular water, especially if grown in pots. They thrive best in rich, well-manured ground that never gets too parched. In a semi-shaded location, hydrangeas sit well among subtle underplantings of short, leafy plants such as *Bergenia*, *Epimedium*, *Pulmonaria*, *Hakonechloa macra*, and ferns.

In a summer border, hydrangeas can make sturdy and reliable anchor plants, bringing dependable quantities of summer bloom, held aloft on strong but flexible stems. They can also make ornamental, billowing hedges, while small cultivars are well suited to growing in pots, provided their water and feeding needs are scrupulously attended to. Gertrude Jekyll was fond of her "tub hydrangeas" standing sentry on either side of her front porch. She also used potted hydrangeas for a process she called "dropping in." These were reserve plants in bloom that she "dropped in" to her flower borders to boost special color effects or fill gaps, just for the duration of their flowering. Afterward, they were smartly moved back to the nursery.

Blue-flowered varieties bloom true when grown in acidic soil, or by using ericaceous potting compost if grown in a container. This still might not be enough to keep them blue (which is a natural reaction to mobile aluminium

ions in the soil). In such cases, there are also proprietary blueing substances, based on aluminum sulfate, which can be used to top up a slightly acidic soil if required. Likewise, reds and pinks are best in alkaline conditions but go toward mauve if their soil pH is acidic, which can be corrected by adding garden lime (i.e., calcium carbonate or ground-up limestone), or calcified seaweed granules. Reestablishing the preferred shade is not immediate but takes a season or two to take effect.

The white, cream, and green-tinted varieties among the *H. paniculata* and *H. arborescens* species are especially lovely when planted where they will light up a shady area and are a great addition to "white"-themed plantings. Perhaps the main event for cream-panicled *H. quercifolia* is supplied by its foliage. This American species has shapely cut leaves resembling the foliage of the red oak tree, naturally giving rise to its popular name, the oak-leaf hydrangea. Also, like its namesake, its foliage glows warmly with burgundy and burnished copper tints before falling in autumn.

For something with slightly wilder ambience, consider *Hydrangea aspera* Villosa Group. These potentially large shrubs, native to the Himalayas, have bristly-velvety leaves and layers of showy, mutable-lilac lacecap flowers. It is the latter that charm, especially when they glow mysteriously at sunset and after. This is thanks to pigments that fluoresce, emitting a gentle, bluish glow as darkness falls. A sheltered location on rich, fertile soil best suits this characterful hydrangea. Grow it where it can do its cabaret act when in summer bloom; afterward, it will retreat discreetly into the background for the months that follow.

→→ As summer begins to give way to autumn: Cottage gardening in containers with a tropical touch, including *Nicotiana sylvestris*, vibrant foliage of coleus, hedychium, canna, agapanthus, and eucomis, ranged around a potted cherry tree at Lowder Mill.

G.T. & A.L. POPE
1959

9 · The Bounty of Autumn

THERE IS A MOMENT IN EARLY AUTUMN WHEN I NEED TO REMEMBER to look up into the sky. We seem to be on a flight path for the swallows that spent their summer in these islands and are now at the beginning of their perilous journey south. On a bright, calm day they fly right overhead, all in one direction, a few here and a few there, in a constant procession. Over the course of a day it amounts to thousands. They will fly some six thousand miles to southern Africa, crossing seas, landmasses, mountains, and the Sahara Desert, risking storms, predators, starvation, and exhaustion, so it is natural to bid them a safe journey.

Because it is a nice day when the swallows start heading for France, there will also be much to do in the garden—hopefully a continuing food harvest—and also a visual feast. The wind swishes about *Miscanthus* stems with their silvery, silken tassels and the sunshine further illuminates the glowing rays of coneflowers (*Rudbeckia* spp.). We do not grow dahlias here—it is too windy for them—but I enjoy them in other people's gardens, in all their great variety. Japanese anemones do really well, however, because their stems are wiry and bendy. No wonder the anemone is called the wind flower.

← Rich golds and reds glow effectively in the soft sunshine of autumn. An imposing arrangement for a sunny bed includes the nonhardy Abyssinian banana plant *Ensete ventricosum* 'Maurelii', *Dahlia* 'Spikey Symbol', *Miscanthus nepalensis*, and dark bronze *Amaranthus* 'Hopi Red Dye'.

↙ A starburst of *Echinacea* 'Harvest Moon'.

→→ Bright gladioli and dahlias in variety, including dahlias 'Ambition' and 'Nuit d'Ete', set off by ethereal blue clouds of *Aster* x *frikartii* 'Monch'.

↑ New England asters, *Symphyotrichum novae-angliae* 'Herbstschnee', 'Andenken an Alma Potschke', and 'Lou Williams', among contrasting wands of Eulalia grass *Miscanthus sinensis* 'Sioux'.

There are usually late flowers on numerous aromatic salvias, on 'Grosso' and 'Phenomenal' lavenders, and wiry-stemmed verbenas, all beloved of the late butterflies and foraging bumblebees. The bumbles craftily reach salvia nectar by drilling a hole close to the base of the flower! Busy spiders make webs everywhere, catching what they can. Bright berries on pyracantha and berberis and the season's rich leaf tints are set off well by 'Little Carlow' asters, the glowing daisies of Michaelmas that seem to change color in different light values.

The Daisies of Michaelmas

One of the plants for which Gertrude Jekyll is exceptionally well known is the Michaelmas daisy, or aster (many of which are now reclassified under the tongue-twisting name of *Symphyoritrichum*). Their popular name arose long ago, from the way these accommodating daisies flower in the period around the time of Michaelmas (September 29), while the title "aster" clearly refers to their starburst daisy flowers, beloved of bees.

Michaelmas daisies contribute enormously to the garden at summer's end and well into autumn. They are not too fussy about sun or partial shade, as long as the soil around their roots is fertile and preferably slightly damp; the one thing they cannot abide is dry and hungry ground. Jekyll, who gardened on the free-draining sandy loam of her Surrey location, got around this drawback by having the copious numbers of plants in her dedicated aster borders at Munstead Wood lifted and divided every year. They were only put back in the ground after the soil had been prepared and enriched with lashings of well-rotted manure that increased the soil's moisture-holding capacity, as well as enriching its nutrient base.

Although asters have long been beloved late-season plants in English gardens, most of the hundreds of hybrids now available, across the spectrum of purples, blues, and pinks, are hybrids that have been bred from species native to the prairies of North America. Asters arrived from the Americas in the sixteenth century and have been cherished ever since, being part of the lexicon of cottage garden flowers for the late season.

Jekyll wrote about Michaelmas daisies many times for, as a color specialist, she continued to experiment with tonal blends and height variations. "The number of kinds good for garden use is now so great that the growers' plant lists are only bewildering, and those who do not know their Daisies should see them in some good nursery or private garden and make their own notes." Her own were:

← A ray of September gold from *Rudbeckia* 'Goldsturm' among the silken tassels of *Miscanthus sinensis* 'Kleine Silberspinne' and foxtail grass *Pennisetum alopercuroides* 'Hameln'.

> carefully but not conspicuously staked with stiff, branching spray cut out the winter before from oaks and chestnuts that have been felled. The spray is put in towards the end of June, when the Asters are making strong growth. The borders are planted and regulated with the two-fold aim of both form and color beauty. In some places rather tall kinds come forward. . . . Each kind is treated at the time of staking according to its own character, and so as best to display its natural form and most obvious use.

Only one other flowering plant was permitted to grow among the Munstead Wood asters, and that was a very tall white-petaled daisy, *Pyrethrum uliginosum* (now called *Chrysanthemum uliginosum*, or *Leucanthemella serotina*). This is the "autumn ox-eye" of old cottage gardens, which later drew the attention of Margery Fish (p. 67), when she moved from London to the countryside. She recalled:

> It is difficult to know what we mean when we talk about a cottage garden plant. It is usually something that is good-tempered and pleasing, quite an ordinary plant that is not particular about soil or position. Some of them are still listed in a few nurserymen's catalogues, but, by degrees they are disappearing and most of us get our odd plants from someone else's garden.
>
> Take, for instance, the tall white daisy once known as *Pyrethrum uliginosum* and now called *Chrysanthemum uliginosum*. Have you ever seen it growing anywhere but in a cottage garden, or listed in a nurseryman's catalogue? I haven't and yet it is a remarkably good plant . . . I noticed it in two cottage gardens when we first came to this village. In one it was grown in a thick row in front of the cabbages and there were not many other things in flower at the time . . . *Chrysanthemum uliginosum* was a new plant to me, and of course I felt I could not live unless I got a bit to grow in my own garden, and I made up my mind to ask for some. I forget now what I gave in exchange, but I hope it was a generous offering.

The imposing white daisy, native to eastern Europe, can reach some six feet tall. Most likely it would have served in the cottage gardens as a companion plant or a source of homemade organic insecticide. Pyrethrums (*Chrysanthemums*) contain compounds that can deal with a range of insect pests including aphids, whiteflies, leafhoppers, and various little beetles. Homemade brews that take advantage of this characteristic go back to ancient times; evidence suggests that certain local species in China were being used to make an organic pyrethrum insecticide some three thousand years ago.

← "Good tempererd and pleasing" cottage garden plants for the late season, including:

CLOCKWISE FROM TOP LEFT:
— Spires of violet *Salvia concolor*
— *Perovskia* garlanded with a spider's web
—*Echinacea purpurea* 'Rubinstern' with *Rudbeckia fulgida* var. Deamii
— *Anemone hupehensis* 'Hadspen Abundance'
— Orange dahlia 'David Howard'
— Dahlia 'Happy Days Pink'

Robinson, Jekyll, and the Arts and Crafts Dynamic

← Detail of Edwin Lutyens's stonework at Hestercombe, Somerset, softened by self-sown Mexican fleabane, *Erigeron karvinskianus*, also known as the Santa Barbara daisy. The superbly restored gardens display the Arts and Crafts love of natural materials, among abundant cottage garden flowers.

A LEADING LIGHT IN THE LATE-NINETEENTH-CENTURY ARTS AND Crafts movement, William Morris (1834–1896) famously declared, "I must have unmistakable suggestions of gardens and fields, and strange trees, boughs, and tendrils, or I can't do with your pattern." He was reacting to the overstuffed drawing rooms of Victorian England and also to the mass-produced goods and factory processes that were taking over from true craftsmanship, owing to the industrial revolution and the importation of cheap goods that had gathered momentum during the earlier half of the century.

Morris chiefly designed interior furnishings, particularly wallpapers and textiles, but his sentiments were echoed outdoors by some of his contemporaries, including gardener and publishing mogul William Robinson (1838–1935) and artist-craftswoman and garden designer Gertrude Jekyll (1843–1932).

Morris drew upon the flowers of the fields, hedgerows, and cottage gardens to inspire his refreshing interior designs. They were ornamented with daisies, columbines (*Aquilegia vulgaris*), snake's head fritillaries (*Fritillaria meleagris*), honeysuckle, and wild roses, among others. Jekyll and Robinson were both prolific writers in the gardening press and similarly promoted a simple approach to gardening itself. Hitherto, with the increasing availability of conservatories in which to cultivate vibrant tender species brought from abroad, formal designs had been created to display them seasonally outdoors. "Ribbon beds" planted in straight lines of contrasting colors and graduated heights, and formal geometric planting patterns designed for beds cut out of the lawn, were very artificial, but believed by many to be the correct way to make a garden in the middle of the nineteenth century. Robinson advocated instead—and loudly—a more natural approach, using hardy shrubs and perennials, and bulbs scattered through the turf to create "natural looking" landscapes. His revolutionary book, *The Wild Garden*, first published in 1870, went to seven editions in his own lifetime and is still in print today.

Jekyll, who was, like Morris, trained in art and design, sought to use hardy plants in harmonic, color-themed borders of herbaceous plants, but she was also influenced and charmed by the approach of country cottage gardeners,

↑ Verbenas, fennel, and white *Cosmos bipinnatus* at Gravetye Manor, Sussex. The mansion (now a hotel) was acquired by "the wild gardener" William Robinson in 1884. As prolific writers of books and magazine articles, Robinson and Jekyll promoted informal, cottage-style planting, a tradition that continues today.

whose simple plantings of assorted things at hand had an honesty and integrity—and often created delightful "pictures."

Both Robinson and Jekyll were very well known and influential gardening authors by the time Edward Hudson, the founder and hands-on proprietor of *Country Life* magazine, launched his new weekly journal at the start of 1897, Queen Victoria's Diamond Jubilee year. Hudson soon engaged both of these already very busy people to write regular gardening articles for *Country Life*, and Jekyll had a steering role in directing the sort of gardening articles the readers would enjoy, as well as contributing features on aspects of country people and cottage life, always a topic close to her heart.

A remarkably talented young architect, Edwin Lutyens (1869–1944) came into the *Country Life* orbit at the close of the nineteenth century and must be mentioned. A generation younger than Jekyll but sharing her enthusiasm for old English vernacular buildings and village life, he was taken under her wing, and their creative partnership is legendary. "A Lutyens house (with gables and tall chimney stacks) with a Jekyll garden" became the signature trophy home for well-heeled patrons with a taste for the Arts and Crafts aesthetic. Outdoors, Lutyens had a gift for creating harmoniously proportioned garden spaces with water rills, playful fountains, generous and geometrically designed stairways, and the all-important Edwardian pergola, for climbing roses and vines. Jekyll created detailed planting plans with herbaceous flowers, old-fashioned roses and some structural accent plants, such as yuccas. Her exuberant flower beds were often margined along the edges with the large-leaved evergreen "elephant's ears," *Bergenia cordifola*, or silvery "lamb's ears," *Stachys lanata*, which gave them a finished and contained look, without being too formal.

The major location for Jekyll's planting experiments was her own home, Munstead Wood, in Surrey, where Lutyens built the house to her specifications—including a workroom for her crafts and a flower room directly connected to the garden, with a sink, work top, and cupboards for assorted vases and other paraphernalia. Munstead Wood was carefully looked after by subsequent owners and has recently been purchased by the National Trust, which will enable access to visitors seeking to learn more about Jekyll.

Robinson's stellar career enabled him to purchase Gravetye Manor, an Elizabethan mansion, in 1884, with its adjacent farms and extensive forest, both of which greatly interested him. Later it became a charming country house hotel and, since 2010, enormous investment has been made in it by the present owners to preserve and build upon Robinson's ideas of "wild gardening" with cultivated plants, alongside all the guest expectations of a leading boutique hotel in lovely countryside.

← The garden at Hestercombe, Somerset: Combining some of the best work of both Lutyens and Jekyll, the garden's layout features playful geometry, overlaid with Jekyll's signature plants, including bergenias, asters, lamb's ears, yuccas, gladioli, and snapdragons.

→→ Autumn arrives in a cherished traditional cottage garden. Flowers tumble over its narrow path, including achilleas, tithonia, coneflowers, persicaria, and cosmos.

10 · Scents and Skeletons of Winter

WITHOUT EVEN PLANNING FOR IT, THE WINTER GARDEN MAY BE FULL of interest—all the more so because there are precious few hours of daylight in which to enjoy it. "Good bones" contribute a lot to the overall aesthetic appeal of a garden at any time, but especially so in winter. Such bones may be provided by shapely shrubs, topiaries, hedges, or individual trees and in a variety of ways.

Evergreens—such as boxwood, holly, yew, *Viburnum tinus*, camellia, laurel—can be planted to form a reliable, permanent framework. Variegated forms of holly, euonymus, and pittosporum are also invaluable at this time, lifting the overall gloom of the season with flashes of cream and gold.

If you prefer to see a greater amount of change in the garden's structure from season to season, plant hedges or topiary pieces fashioned from deciduous beech (*Fagus sylvatica*) or hornbeam (*Carpinus betulus*) that hold onto their curled, brown leaves over the winter. Their russet, bright copper, or chestnut tones contribute an element of seasonal warmth—visually, a sort of sheepskin coat giving texture and depth. In winter, evergreen and deciduous hedges rather usefully provide roosting spaces to shelter birds, with larder attached, as they forage among the twigs, finding morsels of hibernating insects.

For convenience, if we take winter as being the months of December, January, and February, there is no certainty that December will feel truly "wintry," at least in English gardens. Indeed, Christopher Lloyd, who gardened in the mild southeastern corner of England, called early December "the phoney winter, as the season seldom shows its teeth till later on." Depending on how the season shapes up, frosts might be few and far between or of short duration—just enough to make everything sparkle and inspire one to dash indoors to reach for a camera.

Compared with other seasons, winter's flowers are few, but they make a special effort to push out scent to attract the scarce pollinators that may be at large. While the season's blooms individually tend to be small, they may be numerous and deliciously perfumed, as in the shrubby, evergreen Christmas box, *Sarcococca confusa*. What it lacks in floral glamour, it makes up for in punching out a powerful, sweet fragrance. Also in this category we can include the golden

← Topiary figures in beech (*Fagus sylvatica*) are lovely in all seasons, as the leaves develop and change their colors. Holding onto its crumpled and spent foliage through winter, beech contributes warm, rusty tints and ruffled texture to the pared-down landscape.

→→ Sculpted boxwood comes into its own in winter, when herbaceous flowers have been swept away and their roots sit snugly underground. The metal ornaments and endearing shapes provide alternative interest.

bells of wintersweet *Chimonanthus praecox*, a multibranch, deciduous shrub best planted somewhere sunny. On lime-free soil, the Chinese witch hazel, *Hamamelis mollis*, generously wafts its distinctive, spicy-citrus perfume from clusters of tentacle-like, golden flowers from midwinter onward and a few fragrant stems are nice to cut and bring indoors.

Among the pink-petaled perfume-pushers, it is worth making a little space for *Daphne* 'Jacqueline Postill', a small- to medium-sized shrub that can take a while to get established. Once settled in, it rewards you with clusters of sweetly scented, pale-pink stars in the darkest months. Showier is *Prunus* × *subhirtella* 'Autumnalis Rosea', the very hardy "rosebud cherry" tree, which puts out its pretty pink blossoms periodically from autumn to spring, only holding them back during the bleakest periods.

A sprinkling of frost does wonders for shapely spent flowers that have been purposely left in situ for the winter. Last summer's hydrangea blooms are left on our plants to provide added winter protection but they are rather beautiful at this faded stage, in seasonal taupe and tan. Likewise, the spiny, sculptural skeletons of teasel (*Dipsacus fullonum*) are eye-catching. These days, it is considered beneficial to leave the brown seedheads clustered around the moribund stems of *Phlomis russelliana* over the winter, as well as the dark cones on faded

↓ Rose hips may brighten spots in the winter garden, as in this *Rosa* 'Bonica'. They are also welcomed by birds and small rodents as a valuable food source.

echinacea and the flattened, broccoli heads of spent sedums (*Hylotelephium*), such as 'Autumn Joy' and 'Matrona'. All of them contribute to the sepia tints of winter but, more pertinently, provide seed food for a multitude of garden birds.

One of the things I like best about the pared-back state of winter is how easy it is to see the animal life that goes on day to day. A local red fox in his impressive winter coat does his rounds in daylight, looking for anything interesting. Robins, blackbirds, and winter-visiting thrushes from Scandinavia home in on berries of all sorts: the red and then the orange of pyracanthas are eaten first, before yellow ones. Any hips remaining on the roses are much appreciated, as well as crab apples still hanging in the tree. Squirrels dart about, trying to remember where they stashed acorns and other fruits in preceding weeks and months; jays, in their magnificent plumage, do the same. Perhaps they find each other's buried treasures.

Around New Year, when the first snowdrops and crocuses are pushing out of the ground, winter will be with us for at least the next two months (usually longer). But some birds are already tuning up their courting songs and the first flowers on the camellias are starting to open. All in all, there are sure signs that spring is not too far away.

↑ Chinese witch hazel, *Hamamelis mollis*, is one of the best for fragrance and bright golden blooms. It forms a wide-spreading, twiggy shrub with long-lasting flowers opening in the winter, appreciated by the pollinators at large during the season.

→→ Among the skeletons of globe thistles (*Echinops* spp.), white trunks of the birch *Betula utilis* var. *jacquemontii* 'Jermyns' have a sculptural presence.

The Beauty of Birch

Winter is the moment when deciduous trees with attractive bark come to the fore; perhaps chief among them are the multitude of birch species. The white-stemmed Himalayan birches (*Betula utilis* var. *jacquemontii* and its named varieties) have an almost "curated," pristine look and upwardly thrusting branches, a little different in character from the European silver birch, *Betula pendula*. With irregular black clefts bursting through its white bark and lax stems of trailing foliage, the fast-growing silver birch has a slightly "wild forest" ambience that sits well in grassy areas threaded with traditional cottage garden flowers such as foxgloves, dame's violet, columbines, and ox-eye daisies, in due season. Multistemmed versions, where several trunks arise from a common base, can be very attractive where there is space for them.

Pink, caramel, and toffee tones feature in the peeling trunks of *Betula albo-sinensis*, the "red-barked birch" of western China. There is subtlety and warmth in its coloring, while the papery bark is rather special in winter, especially when backlit by the low sun. Birches are seen at their best when they have room to grow naturally, so choose a spot that will give them enough space and will not require hard pruning later on, which often ruins their shape. Birches are fast-growing, "pioneer" species and not as forgiving as some other trees. Pruning should be a last resort and only when they are dormant, to prevent the sap from bleeding and weakening the tree.

11 · The Contained Garden

A HUGE SHIFT IN THE ENJOYMENT OF THE GARDEN AS AN OUTSIDE room has occurred over the past forty-plus years. Container gardening has been a big part of it and contributes a very large section of the nursery trade, with new plants released each year, well suited to pots and planters, as well as cherished classics.

But why use containers at all, if there is already ground to grow plants in? There are numerous reasons, both visual and practical. On the visual side, one might simply want to show off nice pots, further enhancing them with appropriate plants. Or, to highlight a particular part of the garden to make a focal point, or draw the eye to a particular spot, perhaps embellishing a doorway or the top of a flight of steps. There might even be an opportunity to place a pot to one side on the tread of each step, the effect of the planted pots being multiplied by regular repetition. Pots can be arranged together as a collection, to make an interesting and seasonally changing composition. This technique has been perfected over the decades at the Great Dixter garden in East Sussex, with quantities of assorted planted pots arranged to either side of the front door of the house.

On the practical side, container planting has so many benefits. You can grow "special" plants that would not fit in well elsewhere. The mobility of pots (and their contents) enables easy changes for something else—for example, when flowering has finished. Pots enable the creation of special soil conditions different from the garden soil. Today, specialist potting mixes are widely available in garden stores and other outlets, for every conceivable plant need. For instance, acid-loving plants such as azaleas and camellias can be potted into ready-made ericaceous (lime-free) compost; succulents can be grown successfully in a fast-draining, gritty soil mix to make potted confections for the summer that bring an exotic, warm climate ambience. *Aeoniums*, native to the mild-climate islands of Macaronesia, have become especially popular in this respect, as well as tender but geometrically compelling *Echeveria*, aloes, and the hardier *Sempervivums*, or houseleeks. Species with large foliage character, such as hostas, cannas, strelitzia, and the "tractor seat plant" *Farfugium japonicum* can

← Pretty in pinks: The purple poppy mallow or buffalo rose of the Great Plains, *Callirhoe involucrata*, pink evening primrose *Oenothera speciosa*, and autumn sage *Salvia greggii* 'Salvito Scarlet' sit well together in a rustic container.

→→ A snug sheltered terrace is ideal for displaying a container collection. Repetition of the key plants creates a unified picture; they include dark bronze *Aeonium* 'Zwartkop', bold-leaved *Hosta sieboldiana* var. *elegans*, and its variegated version, *H. s.* 'Frances Williams'.

↑ An old stone trough, with custom engraving for its location, contains Viola 'Nora' and contrasting *Acaena inermis* 'Purpurea'.

→ Cottage style for spring: Assorted Darwin Hybrid tulips and orange wallflowers fill out a large pot, alongside smaller pots of tulips, including 'Blue Diamond' and 'Angelique'

contribute a wonderfully lush, tropical ambience, enjoyable to sit among on the terrace, where their splendid beauty can be appreciated at eye level.

Sometimes, growing in pots is the only way to bring plants to an outdoor space; typical cases would include a balcony, a paved patio, a windowsill, or a rooftop terrace. There are so many advantages to container gardening—not least of them is that no digging in the ground is required! There is also less chance of pest damage, since the plants are already elevated away from the soil and are easily looked over and checked for such things. Growing plants in containers, whether seasonally or year-round, enables them to receive a special feed routine according to their needs, and likewise, a specific watering regime. This regular care is actually their chief maintenance concern and requires the greatest focus, for potted plants are completely dependent upon you for their ability to thrive or to perish.

A Potted History of Gardening in Pots

→ CLOCKWISE, FROM TOP LEFT:

— Mix-and-match chrysanthemums in decorative ironwork

— Contrasting foliage and pots on a table of varied succulents

— *Erigeron karvinskianus* and *Campanula portenschlagiana* share a pot

— Zinc buckets display a collection of scented-leaf pelargoniums, with silver plectranthus

— Lavender in a copper pot

— Assorted size pots for a collection of foliage contrasts

Container gardening is probably as old as gardening itself, with archaeological discoveries of pots having been in some form of horticultural usage among the ancient societies in China, Mesopotamia (modern-day Iraq), and Egypt.

The Romans used a wide variety of pots, often decorated, which served numerous purposes. Pliny the Elder mentioned pots "with breathing holes for the roots" being used for acclimatizing imported lemon trees. Pots of baked clay, terra-cotta, have been the most widely used kind across the centuries, whether plain, ornamented with materials such as stones and shells, or glazed and patterned. In due course and with improved technology, stone and metal containers came to be increasingly used as well. Wood also came into use, especially fashioned into circular tubs like barrels, held together with metal hoops. Square wooden tubs were developed into models with removable sides—Versailles planters—in the seventeenth century, again for the transportation of citrus trees.

Various cultures enjoy renown for particular methods of container cultivation; the modern cottage gardener draws inspirations from any and all. A floral tradition in the European Alps has long been the display of pelargoniums spilling over balcony troughs at the windows of alpine chalets throughout the summer. The patios (mainly enclosed courtyards) of Córdoba, in the south of Spain, are famous for their displays of flowers in flat-backed "half-pots," fixed all over the courtyard walls (requiring, of course, devotion to regular watering).

The industrial revolution of the nineteenth century saw greatly increased production of pots in numerous shapes, patterns, and materials. The Victorian gardener Gertrude Jekyll, champion of all things to do with cottage life and gardens, had much to say about container gardening. "Good groupings of smaller plants in pots is a form of ornament that might be made more use of in our own gardens, especially where there are paved spaces near a house." She recommended hostas, aspidistras, ferns, hydrangeas, and lilies (*Lilium longiflorum* and *L. speciosum*) for a shady courtyard. In a sunny spot, more potted lilies, plus hydrangeas, cannas, and especially "Geraniums" (*Pelargonium*) flowering in her preferred shades of soft pink, rosy-scarlet, and salmon-red.

Writer Mirabel Osler (1925–2016) recalled in her celebrated memoir *A Gentle Plea for Chaos*, the petunias she had seen grown in India:

> Petunias, in particular, looked wonderful in the imaginative way in which pots were grouped in concentric circles, on three low tiers. Shades of mulberry, heliotrope, ultramarine, and amethyst were arranged, one circle within the other, into floral domes; some were carmine, madder, scarlet and clashing magenta, others were rings of topaz and lemon, highlighted by pots of pure white. Set amongst the deep shadows of citrus trees and patches of brilliant sunlight, these graduated mounds appeared as huge, semi-precious ornaments.

↘ A classic window box for summer, filled with cascading ivy-leaved pelargoniums.

→ Magenta and white fuchsia, blue lobelia, calibrachoa, and ivy-leaf pelargoniums, including two-toned 'Rouletta'.

It is a good reminder of the bold and cheerful effects that can be achieved from the petunia, one of the all-time most popular bedding plants.

Garden petunias (*Petunia* × *hybrida*, or *P.* × *atkinsiana*) are hybrids derived from species native to South America. Being members of the *Solanaceae*, the tobacco family, they have kinship with other very familiar plants, such as tomatoes, peppers, and chiles all of which also make great container plants, of course, albeit having different qualities as far as decorative merit is concerned.

A worthy challenger to the ever-popular, decorative petunia is one of its close relatives, *Calibrachoa*, also known as Million Bells, or Superbells. While having similar flower shape and by now an even greater color range, *Calibrachoa* blooms are smaller than petunias, but extremely plentiful, borne on stems with a trailing growth habit, ideal for spilling over pots, window boxes, and hanging baskets. They also tend to shed their spent flowers easily, thus removing the need for deadheading to maintain a long season of flower production.

Another currently strong trend in container gardening is the curated display of succulents, albeit best suited to regions where it is more likely to be sunny than rainy. These otherworldly desert plants look wonderful grouped together to show off a range of shapes, leaf colors, and textures. A small collection for an outdoor tabletop display is not too difficult to rush under cover, if the weather turns inclement. Succulents are especially amenable to being grown in shallow bowls, including unusual and decorative ones, given a fast-draining blend of 50:50 medium-rich potting mix and fine grit. In the British Isles, where there are likely to be more cold and/or rainy days in summer than hot, dry ones, the succulent effect is more safely achieved with hardy species, such as stonecrops (*Sedum*/*Hylotelephium* spp.), and *Sempervivum* (hen-and-chicks).

Choosing Containers

↑ Harmony from repetition: 'Apricot Beauty' tulips in terra-cotta, for an uplifting spring display.

Bearing in mind that container gardening can be time consuming, carefully choosing the best pot for the job can mean less work. It is worth remembering that the larger the pot, the more soil it will hold; therefore, the soil in large pots tends to dry out less quickly, enabling plant roots more freedom to grow and develop the bits we like to see above the surface.

With any pots, straight sided, or "vase shaped," i.e., wider at the top than the bottom, are the best choice for anything likely to be kept long term, such as shrubs or small trees, which will need to be repotted at some stage into a bigger container. This is because the root ball will need to be lifted out cleanly, without being obstructed by an inwardly curved rim, or a shouldered shape that narrows toward the top. You do not want to have to smash the pot to get the root ball out! Pots that are curved inward at the top are perfectly fine, however, for annual bedding plants, seasonal bulbs, or anything temporary that will not be making a big root ball over the long term.

Terra-cotta, the most ancient of pot materials, has natural affinity with the garden setting. There are many beautiful designs, and some terra-cotta pots are guaranteed to be frostproof, though most are not. Terra-cotta pots are heavy to move and, since they are made from porous clay, they need more frequent watering than any other material. Sometimes it can be useful to coat the inside with a nontoxic all-purpose primer to seal it and enable moisture to stay within the soil for longer.

Well-made wooden containers, such as half barrels and cuboid, or Versailles styles, have a natural, attractive appearance, well suited to a country or cottage garden setting. They also have weight, which makes them useful in windy areas and for securely nurturing top-heavy plants.

Glazed earthenware and ceramic pots can be very attractive and bring extra visual interest into the arrangement as a whole. They are fragile, however, and many are not frostproof. Glazed pots are well suited to temporary, summer bedding arrangements, which will be cleaned out before winter. They are also good for displaying succulents or dwarf seasonal bulbs—but be sure to find pots with drainage holes in the bottom, which not all of them have.

Metal containers are made in both traditional castings and unfussy, modern designs for a clean, streamlined look. They can look very stylish, but they have poor insulation, meaning they can get hot in the summer, which is not always helpful to the plant roots contained within. Corten steel, admired for its rusted patina, has become very popular for strong, refined containers in recent times. It is also known as weathering steel, being a type of steel alloy that naturally develops a protective, rust-like patina when exposed to the elements. It can be quite a pleasing, natural shade seen against the greenery of plants. The patina is said to stabilize and inhibit further corrosion, making it durable and maintenance-free.

There are advantages and disadvantages to plastic pots. They are lightweight and easy to move and also inexpensive. Some plastic pots can become brittle after exposure to sunlight, but they are frostproof. They can be made more interesting and attractive by painting the exterior (first, apply a universal primer base coat, to make the painted top coat adhere). In this way, it is possible to achieve a stylish, curated look, even on a tight budget.

← Glazed ceramic pots bring extra visual interest, planted here with *Bellis perennis* daisies for spring.

→→ A multitude of late-summer dahlias, beside sweet peas and box-edged beds. Dahlias with open centers, revealing the central yellow disc of working parts, are very attractive to pollinators.

12 · Plants for Pollinators

THE ROLE OF POLLINATING INSECTS IS PROFOUND. ON ONE LEVEL, there is, of course, the pleasure of seeing busy bees at work and dainty butterflies flitting about; they reinforce the feeling of an ecosystem going on in one's own plot. And without pollinators, it would be very difficult to get any harvest out of the fruit and vegetable plants we grow. Since they are rooted into the ground, plants depend on either the wind to disperse their pollen or, more often, insects that crawl over the anthers, gathering pollen on their bodies that they spread to other flowers as they move about, enabling the process of fruit and seed development.

Statistics suggest alarming population decline among pollinating insects around the world, and the reasons for this are various, including dramatic changes in agricultural methods over the past seventy years and more widespread use of pesticides. Likewise, in the middle of the twentieth century, advertisements for garden chemicals propagated the point of view that insects were a foe with which we must do battle. Rather strong chemicals and powders were freely available that probably worked for certain garden pests but indiscriminately killed others that are crucial to the overall health and productivity of the garden and to other wildlife.

Thankfully, the most damaging chemicals have since been banned; people are wiser now and you do not have to look very far to find out which plants are really good at attracting pollinating insects. Frequently, I find that the labels on plants at garden stores indicate when a plant is a good attractor for creatures such as hoverflies, bees, and butterflies, and many nursery websites are good at highlighting this too. When you look closely at the flowers in your garden, all sorts of creatures perform the invaluable role of transferring pollen. As well as the "pretty" ones, the same good service may be done by assorted moths, flies, wasps, and beetles. Wasps, particularly, have a bad reputation, partly from their annoying, uninvited participation in our outdoor parties and picnics (with the possibility of nasty stings). When you grow to like wasps, however, you see them as allies that do tremendous service in eating up a lot of soft-bodied pests, particularly aphids, of which they will eat thousands!

← Honeybees love the flowers of *Ornithogalum* spp., also known as the Star of Bethlehem. The blooms of these bulbs are a reliable source of both pollen and nectar.

→→ Small tortoiseshell butterflies forage among flowers of *Allium* 'Summer Beauty'. Alliums are attractive to numerous pollinating insects, having dense, globe-shaped flower heads comprising numerous individual flowers, each containing nectar for energy and protein-rich pollen.

SOME FLOWERING PLANTS FOR POLLINATORS

A = annual; B = bulb; Bi = biennial; C = climber; H = herbaceous; S = shrub (For more pollinator plants, see also: Wild Things: prairie plants, p. 175 and Herbs, p. 235.)

SPRING

- *Arabis alpina* subsp. *caucasica*, alpine rock cress H
- *Armeria caespitosa*, juniper-leaved thrift H
- *Aubrieta*, various, aubretia H
- *Aurinia saxatilis*, gold dust H
- *Berberis thunbergii* Japanese barberry S
- *Campanula* spp. bellflower H
- *Ceanothus* spp. California lilac S
- *Crocus* spp. crocus (spring-flowering) B
- *Erica* spp. Heath—hardy types S
- *Erysimum* spp. wallflower Bi or H
- *Helleborus* × *hybridus*, hellebore H
- *Hyacinthus orientalis*, common hyacinth B
- *Iberis sempervirens*, perennial candytuft H
- *Muscari* spp. (several), grape hyacinth B
- *Ornithogalum* spp. (several) B
- *Primula* spp., several H
- *Pulmonaria* spp. lungwort H
- *Ribes sanguineum* flowering currant S
- *Scilla siberica*, Siberian squill B
- *Skimmia japonica*, skimmia S

SUMMER

- *Agastache* spp. giant hyssop H
- *Armeria maritima*, thrift H
- *Astrantia major*, greater masterwort H
- *Betonica officinalis*, betony H
- *Borago officinalis*, borage A
- *Buddleja davidii*, butterfly bush S
- *Calamintha nepeta*, lesser calamint H
- *Calendula officinalis*, common marigold A
- *Calluna vulgaris*, summer heather S
- *Centranthus ruber* red valerian H
- *Cirsium rivulare* Atropurpureum, plume thistle
- *Echinops* spp. globe thistle H
- *Erigeron* spp. fleabane H
- *Eschscholzia californica* California poppy A
- *Foeniculum vulgare* common fennel H
- *Dianthus barbatus* sweet william Bi
- *Digitalis purpurea*, common foxglove Bi
- *Nepeta* spp. catmint H
- Paeonia spp. peony H
- *Hyssopus officinalis*, hyssop S
- *Iberis amara*, wild candytuft A
- *Origanum marjorana*, sweet marjoram S
- *Penstemon* spp. beard-tongue H
- *Phacelia tanacetifolia*, blue tansy, fiddleneck A
- *Knautia macedonica* Macedonian scabious H
- *Phlox paniculata* perennial phlox H
- *Lavandula* spp. lavender S
- *Limnanthes douglasii* poached egg flower A
- *Lobularia maritima* sweet alyssum A
- *Lonicera periclymenum*, honeysuckle Cl
- *Salvia* spp. sage A or H
- *Scabiosa* spp. scabious A/H
- *Matthiola incana*, Brompton stock Bi
- *Stachys byzantina* lamb's ears H
- *Tagetes patula* French marigold A

AUTUMN

- *Anemone* × *hybrida* Japanese anemone H
- *Verbena bonariensis* purple top H
- *Ceratostigma plumbaginoides* hardy blue-flowered leadwort H
- *Chrysanthemum* spp. chrysanthemum H
- *Colchicum* spp, autumn crocus B
- *Erica* spp. heath – hardy types S
- *Eryngium* spp. eryngo, sea holly H
- *Hedera* spp. ivy C
- *Helianthus* spp. sunflower A or H
- *Malva* spp. mallow H
- *Salvia* spp. sage (autumn-flowering types) H
- *Sedum* (*Hylotelephium*) Autumn Joy P

WINTER

- *Chionodoxa luciliae*, glory of the snow B
- *Cornus mas* Cornelian cherry S
- *Crocus* spp. crocus (winter-flowering) B
- *Erica arborea*, E. carnea (winter heather) S
- *Galanthus nivalis* common snowdrop B
- *Helleborus niger*, Christmas rose, H
- *Lonicera fragrantissima* winter honeysuckle S
- *Mahonia* spp. Oregon grape S
- *Narcissus* 'February Gold', daffodil B
- *Narcissus* 'Tete-a-Tete', daffodil
- *Sarcococca* spp. sweet box S
- *Viburnum tinus*, laurustinus S

When your eye is attuned, it is easy to see which plants have a beneficial role to play for pollinators and which do not. Plants with "single flowers" are magnets for many foraging flyers.

If you grow peonies, for example, be sure to include some of the more open-bloomed species and varieties, such as 'Bowl of Beauty', 'Coral Charm', 'Buckeye Belle', among numerous others, including the woody-stemmed types (often called "tree peonies"), such as the *Paeonia rockii* hybrids. They show their yellow stamens, the working parts of the flower that the bees are after. The big, blowsy peonies that are very dense with petals look wonderful to us, of course, but that very density means the insects cannot reach inside the bloom.

It is certainly worth growing plenty of pollinator-friendly flowers among vegetables and fruiting plants; they are like the advertising posters at a mall, beckoning passersby to "come in and take a look around." Fragrant and flowering herbs, especially lavender, chives, rosemary, thymes, and sages are irresistible. Bees also enjoy annual nasturtiums, which are not only incredibly easy to grow, but can serve several uses. Nasturtiums look wonderful in flower and have attractive leaves; the edible flowers look pretty in salads, but these plants may also be used as a "sacrificial crop," attracting certain butterflies that would otherwise lay their eggs on your brassicas. The resulting caterpillars munching away on nasturtiums can then be removed, along with aphids, another pest magnetically drawn to these flamboyant flowers, instead of the crops you want for yourself.

Low-growing and floriferous sweet alyssum (*Lobularia maritima*), a traditional flower of cottage gardens, is rich in nectar and wafts around its sweet honey scent and especially attractive to all manner of butterflies, including glamorous species such as the swallowtails and peacocks. The migrating painted lady and hummingbird hawk moths (both native to southern Europe and North Africa), who do not always visit English gardens—unless there is settled weather for their travels and a good, warm summer—find lavender and sweet alyssum to be like Michelin-starred restaurants, welcoming their arrival and proffering irresistible menus. Sweet alyssum is also appreciated by North America's famous fluttering migrant the monarch butterfly; this is a flower that seems to be universally enjoyed in the butterfly world.

Wild foxgloves are emblematic cottage garden flowers of early summer and magnets for long-tongued bees such as the common carder and bumblebees. As children, we enjoyed picking off the foxglove flowers to put one on each finger, in the age-old way, but soon learned to check first to see if a bee was already lurking in the tubular flower. Other tubular flowers adored by bees include honeysuckles, jasmines, penstemons, and fuchsias.

Flattened, multiple flower heads, as seen on verbenas, yarrow (*Achillea* spp.), fennel, parsley, and a whole range of umbellifers are easy for hoverflies to settle on, like helicopters on a landing pad, and butterflies also find them easy to visit. The onion family, embracing ornamental alliums as well as chives, leeks, garlic,

and their ilk, provides a globular feast of tiny, nectar-rich flowers, equally enthusiastically foraged. Honeybees enjoy all of these too, but the species they seem to enjoy most of all throughout summer is *Calamintha nepeta*, or lesser calamint, a small perennial herb in the mint family. Growing about fifteen inches (38 cm) tall, its mound of soft leaves (which pleasingly look and smell like mint) produce little spires of tiny flowers that individually are so small and pale that they seem insignificant—but the honeybees hereabouts ignore most other things, even, to some extent, their beloved lavenders and marjorams, if there is calamint around.

When planting the garden for pollinators, not just summer but all seasons must be kept in mind, since some creatures will be at large in autumn and winter, and many more again in the spring. By planting snowdrops and fragrant winter-flowering shrubs, there will always be something of interest for the wildlife. Spring brings with it an abundance of blossoms and bulbs. Among the best all-around pollinator flowers for autumn include sedums (stonecrops), hebes, and wild ivy (*Hedera helix*) whose nectar-rich flowers later develop dark berries, enjoyed by a number of garden birds.

↑ Hyacinth bulbs are capable of pumping powerful fragrance into the spring air, announcing to local bees that the "restaurant is now open." *Hyacinthus orientalis* comes in a multitude of colors and can be grown in the open ground or, more popularly, in pots. Choose simple-flowered ones, like these, which enable pollinators easy access to feed.

13 · Inspired by Prairie and Meadow

FOR DECADES, THERE HAS BEEN A GENERAL SHIFT TOWARD MAKING our gardens, great and small, more wildlife friendly—even a little more "wild" looking. Current trends are for looser, less prescriptive approaches to planting than were enjoyed just a couple of generations ago. The cottage-inspired prairie look exudes quite a bucolic atmosphere, being visited throughout the summer by spectacular moths, bees, butterflies, and birds. Perhaps it is accessed by the rest of us via rustic paths of shredded bark or mowed turf, between plants such as the wild pink *Dianthus carthusianorum* and wild carrots (*Daucus carota*) peeping above longer grass; or American prairie species, such as coneflowers (*Rudbeckia* spp.), asters, prairie sunflower (*Helianthus petiolaris*), and goldenrod (*Solidago* spp.).

Taking a broad-brush look at some key influences, one would need to include the much-grander-scale work of landscape architects Wolfgang Oehme and James van Sweden from the mid-1970s onward, with their "New American Garden" style, characterized by large swaths of grasses and herbaceous perennials, in a flowing, faux-natural style. Their approach has focused on creating low-maintenance ecosystems, rejecting the use of pesticides and other chemicals and reducing the sort of water needs that formal, more traditional approaches tend to require. Likewise, a similar "new perennials" movement in Europe gathered pace in the late twentieth century, with identical aims and considerable crossover in plant species used, particularly with ornamental grasses. All of the above built considerably upon the mid-century plant breeding work of pioneers such as Karl Foerster and George Arends in Germany and Alan Bloom in England.

Contemporary with those movements was a greater interest in Britain's own wild plant communities, particularly the flora of meadows, a much-diminished part of the agricultural landscape. Various influencers of the time included the late Marchioness of Salisbury (1922–2016) who restored and re-created native wildflower meadows in several locations; and florist-turned-nurserywoman Beth Chatto, in Essex (1923–2018), who focused on the different habitats in her garden to experiment with both wild and cultivated plants. Chatto wrote about them in books such as *The Damp Garden*, *The Dry Garden*, and *Beth Chatto's Gravel Garden* (recently reissued as *Drought Resistant Planting*).

← Prairie in miniature: A cottage garden path, lined with white sagebrush *Artemisia ludoviciana*, feather grass *Stipa tenuissima*, dark red hollyhocks, and rose campion *Lychnis* (*Silene*) *coronaria*.

↑ Among assorted grasses, red-hot pokers (*Kniphofia* spp.), *Thalictrum* delavayi 'Album', and bronze-leaved *Lobelia speciosa* bring a wild look to this cottage garden.

→ Late summer in bloom, with blue asters, coneflowers 'Prairie Blazing Star' *Liatris pychnostachya*, and the "rattlesnake master" *Eryngium yuccifolium*.

→→ Over in the meadow (where the tall grass grew) . . . *Monarda* 'Kardinal', *Nepeta subsessilis*, *Agastache* 'Blackadder', and *Calamagrostis* grasses blend beautifully.

One might reasonably ask, "What has any of that 'grand scale' approach got to do with cottage gardens?" The answer is, quite a lot. On the one hand, it somewhat revisits the mid-nineteenth-century Arts and Crafts intentions of William Morris, Gertrude Jekyll, and William Robinson (p. 141). Much of Morris's most successful work celebrates England's wild flora and exploited the design potential that emerged when simple cottage garden flowers were examined (something also very close to Jekyll's heart). The work of Robinson, the original "wild gardener" preempts, in various ways, late twentieth-century ecological planting styles, including creating "natural" scenes with drifts of spring bulbs and wildflowers erupting out of meadow grass. Such influences as these have inevitably woven into the genre of country cottage gardening via, of course, the skills and creativity of each garden's maker. Garden shows, not least the annual RHS Chelsea Flower Show in London, have revealed over the past couple of decades how well this approach to planting can be adapted to suit even very tiny gardens and urban locations.

SOME PLANTS FOR THE PRAIRIE GARDEN LOOK

Daisies

- *Anthemis tinctoria*
- *Echinacea purpurea*
- *Helenium*
- *Helianthus*
- *Rudbeckia*
- *Symphoritrichum (aster) laeve*
- *Symphoritrichum (aster) novae-angliae*

Spires

- *Echium russicum*
- *Eremurus*
- *Liatris spicata*
- *Lythrum salicaria*
- *Salvia nemorosa*
- *Salvia pratensis*
- *Verbascum*
- *Veronicastrum virginicum*

Umbellifers
(umbrellalike structured flower heads)

- *Achillea* 'Galaxy Series'
- *Angelica archangelica*
- *Angelica* 'Ebony'
- *Anthriscus sylvestris*
- *Cenolophium denudatum*
- *Chaerophyllum hirsutum* 'Roseum'
- *Eryngium agavifolium*
- *Foeniculum vulgare* 'Purpureum'
- *Pimpinella major* 'Rosea'

And also . . .

- *Allium sphaercephalon*
- *Dianthus carthusianorum*
- *Hemerocallis*
- Iris sibirica
- *Knautia macedonica*
- *Linum perenne*
- *Oenothera*
- *Thalictrum*
- Verbena bonariensis

Tall grasses

- *Calamagrostis*
- *Miscanthus sinensis*
- *Panicum virgatum*
- *Stipa gigantea*

Not-so-tall grasses

- *Anemanthele lessoniana* (aka *Stipa arundinacea*)
- *Deschampsia caespitosa*
- *Hakonechloa macra*
- *Melica altissima* 'Alba'
- *Molinia caerulea*
- *Pennisetum alopercurioudes*
- *Stipa tenuissima*

Early- to mid-spring is a good time for planting a prairie-style plot, which need not be large. Choose plants according to your soil type, local weather conditions, and how much direct sunlight is available. Most of the classic perennial prairie plants and grasses are completely hardy and thrive in average, free-draining soils in a bright, open location; some are more tolerant of shade. Think of it as planting a flower border but more loosely, with ornamental grasses stitched in.

During the emergent and flowering season from mid-spring to autumn, the look is quite casual, in harmony with modern sentiment to encourage wildlife with little interference from the gardener. Nevertheless, these places are not low maintenance. Plants, including grasses, left to their own devices set and scatter their seeds and some can take over. Seeds of other species will surely arrive and settle, either with the help of the wind, or passing animals and birds. Things can get "too wild" with unwanted thistles, docks, and sapling trees stealthily emerging among summer's floral abundance. The answer is to cut everything back severely before the end of each year and remove interlopers. In early and mid-spring, fresh weeds become apparent and need pulling out before the main event of the summer flowers takes over. Some will be missed or will appear later, requiring further removal from time to time.

← The purple coneflower, *Echinacea purpurea* 'Pink Glow'.

↑ Wild things: *Dianthus carthusianorum*, *Echinacea paradoxa*, and *Penstemon barbatus*.

→→ A thematic range of pinks and creams, including *Astrantia major*, *Lythrum salicaria* 'Blush', *Verbena bonariensis*, *Veronicastrum virginicum* 'Adoration', and *Cephalaria gigantea*.

14 · Making a Feature of Water

> We are now about to enter an entirely new world, as different as the one which Alice entered when she stepped through the looking-glass. The simile is not inapt, for we too shall be stepping, in imagination, through a mirrored surface . . . the surface of a pool; nor will it be only on our imagination that we shall be relying, for we shall be able to see, quite clearly, the strange life that unfolds itself below, the fantastic creatures that glide and dart through the green shadows, the curious stems and roots that weave and wave, like fingers groping.
>
> — BEVERLEY NICHOLS

IT IS NOT NECESSARY, OF COURSE, TO HAVE FISH OR AMPHIBIANS swimming about as part of the experience of water in the garden. Indeed, water features of one kind or another can be fitted into the smallest of outdoor spaces as well as the largest, as the following examples will show; but there is one incontrovertible truth: Water's presence can enable plants to survive and thrive, bringing forth life.

Manipulation of water via channels, aqueducts, and fountains was worked out by ancient civilizations many millennia ago. For them, water was not just functional; it was associated with life, abundance, and the divine. The Persians learned from the Egyptians and other civilizations how to harness water and create oasis-like environments known as *pairidaiza*, the paradise garden. In an arid and harsh environment, a well-considered water feature brings the possibility of coolness and shade in summer's heat, plus an abundance of fruit and the fragrance and beauty of flowers.

Russell Page noted that in the Persian city of Isfahan, in the late 1940s:

> Every house had a shady garden of plane trees, poplars, quinces and hazelnuts which shade great bushes of single yellow, orange and scarlet sweetly scented roses. A tiny, stepped canal runs down the middle of the plane-shaded *chaharbagh*, perhaps the world's loveliest processional way, and almost every garden is set symmetrically round a central pool whose four subsidiary rills carry water into each quarter of the garden and then to the roots of every tree and plant.

← The scarlet *Geum* 'Blazing Sunset' stoops to admire its own reflection in this two-tiered pond.

→→ Perfectly contained for a small outdoor space: A zinc water trough, joined by 'Jan van Leeuwen' peonies, ferny *Selinum wallichianum*, and round-leaved *Asarum europaeum*.

↑ "Not only a mirror but a magnet . . . it can pluck the moon from the sky and float it like a lily. . . ." An old stone trough brings reflections to a patio.

→ Lively with multiple jets, fountain and pool designs of this kind go back into the mists of time and may be small enough for courtyards. *Anemone* x *hybrida* contributes to its relaxed feel.

Page considered these timeless Persian plots with their piled-in mixtures of florals, edibles, and herbs the ancestors of the traditional cottage yard. "Nearest to them in feeling are the English cottagers' gardens, where a similar mixture of plants were and still are crowded close to the house within easy reach of the kitchen door and the rainwater butt."

Playful fountains and gurgling rills have been popular in formal garden designs, both monastic and grandiose ever since, but it was during the golden age of the Edwardian Arts and Crafts garden that fountains and rills became linked to relaxed cottage garden planting, notably in designs resulting from the partnership of Edwin Lutyens and Gertrude Jekyll. Indeed, among her early travels, Jekyll experienced firsthand the Moorish fountain courtyards in Algiers when visiting in 1873.

The quiet, still pool offers a different energy from that of sparkling fountains and active, running water, romantically summed up by Beverley Nichols:

> It is not only a mirror but a magnet, with a power that reaches to the ends of space. It can pluck the moon from the sky and float it like a lily; it can reach up to the dark night to draw down the stars and hold them shining to its breast; and through all the

> seasons it paints its pictures of the flowers that lean over it; the steely engravings of the snowdrops on some grey day of February; the rich flush of the lilacs in May, the blood-red ripples that it catches from the maples in October.

Furthermore, a still pool can itself have many different applications and themes. Stepping stones may be laid across it, to invite a close relationship with the water. An attractive metal or stone tank in the garden may double as a handy source for irrigating nearby plants when required, if a watering can is parked close by. Water lilies enjoy the stillness of a pond on which to open their exotic flowers and spread out their circular pads. The latter make convenient landing places for resting dragonflies, frogs and toads, or foraging moorhens.

Some people insist that every garden needs water, and indeed, there are plenty of fountains, miniature ponds, carved-out chunks of stone, and perfectly shaped circular bowls for sale that would fit neatly into the smallest patio garden or on a terrace, where wild birds may drop by for a quick drink or a feather-cleaning bath. However, other considerations should be weighed before absolutely committing to something large. The eminent garden designer John Brookes (1933–2018) cautioned:

> I do not subscribe to the theory that every garden needs water. In a northern climate particularly, I think water can be very depressing between October and April, with the accompanying dead vegetation, floating leaves and defence system necessary to keep predators from eating the fish. . . . Where water is desired by a client, I prefer large simple sheets of it in the country, and a structured pool, preferably raised, containing a small mass of water in an urban area.

The Swimming Pond

If the concept of wild swimming appeals to you, being able to do so on your own doorstep might have considerable allure. Where there is space to create one, a swimming pond can be an attractive feature particularly well suited to level ground, with the benefits of being chemical free and in a seminatural environment.

Swimming ponds might be thought of as hybrids between a traditional swimming pool and a natural garden pond. The complete area consists of two equally sized parts: a pool of fresh water deep enough to swim in, contained by a wall whose top surface sits some eight inches (20 cm) or so below the water's surface. The walled swimming area is surrounded by a submerged bed of aquatic marginal plants, known as the regeneration area, which forms an important part of a biological filtration process.

To get crystal clear and healthy swimming water, the whole system depends upon a pump working twenty-four hours a day, which filters all of the pool water through the planted zone and a filtration system of gravels and pipework lying beneath it. Water is drawn down through the biological filter and, once cleaned, is pumped back into the swimming area. There is no heating, of course, because the plants and the creatures that live among them need to survive.

Swimming ponds are not low maintenance; fallen leaves need to be skimmed off the surface, along with regular clearing of sludge from the pond floor. All of the stems and foliage of plants in the regeneration area need to be cut right back to base and removed at the start of winter at which time the water area doubles, since the regeneration zone is submerged. At such a time, the pond may indeed "pluck the moon from the sky and float it like a lily" or draw down the stars, just as Nichols anticipated.

← In summer, the abundance of herbaceous flowers conceals the source of this tiny pond and water jet. Plants include a dogwood tree, *Cornus kousa*, *Astrantia major*, *Hakonechloa macra* grass, purple irises, and pale blue *Amsonia tabernaemontana* var. *salicifolia*.

↓ The deeper swimming area of a swimming pond is surrounded by a submerged bed of aquatic marginal plants (such as *Lythrum salicaria*, waterlilies and *Pontederia cordata*). They form part of a biological filtration process.

→→ Combining the rows of vegetables and seasonal flowers such as cosmos and yarrow, this cherished traditional cottage garden is the model of productivity and industrious activity.

15 · Top Vegetables

PRIOR TO THE SEVENTEENTH CENTURY, THE DAILY DIET FOR MANY people was severely limited and prone to the vagaries of the weather. Grain crop failures were common, and Chaucer informed us of the limited diet of a medieval cottage dweller (p. 23), which was bland and basic, although she raised meat and dairy produce for others.

In the sixteenth and seventeenth centuries, foreign adventures and exploration introduced new edible plants to Europe with tomatoes, beans, potatoes, maize, and squashes being brought back from the Americas. Nevertheless, for a while, various of these newfangled species were considered curiosities and were only familiar to the upper echelon of society. When the first documented tomatoes were recorded in Europe in the sixteenth century, they were thought to be unusual and interesting just as ornamental plants. They were also believed to be poisonous; John Gerard positively disliked "their ranke and stinking" toxic leaves and "corrupt" fruit.

Plant exchanges and introductions were followed by development of the greenhouse as a means of raising and keeping warm-climate species alive. These factors and the subsequent development of refrigeration have all helped expand the dietary repertoire and made gardening much more rewarding. After growing, there is the pleasure of harvesting the produce you raised from seed and taking it straight to the kitchen to prepare or preserve.

For a number of crops, especially salad greens, sowing small quantities at staged intervals enables successive harvests over the maximum possible period. Getting the timing right for sowing, planting, tending, and harvesting becomes second nature quite quickly. For anyone new to growing their own produce, I suggest herbs, salad greens, tomatoes, and peppers to start with. They are fairly quick to give results and easy to grow in small spaces, including containers. There is nothing like success to encourage further exploration into becoming even partly self-sufficient. Fruit trees and bushes are also extremely worthwhile because, once established, they keep on producing year after year.

← Vibrant and edible: Red cabbages, onions, beets, chards, and potatoes in a thriving plot. Getting the timing right for sowing, planting, tending, and harvesting becomes second nature quite quickly

All About Raised Beds

Even from a purely aesthetic point of view, the raised bed can have many advantages. Regular, rectangular beds laid out in a grid pattern bring visual order, especially during periods of chaotic bounty, when the growing season is in full swing.

An arrangement of beds can provide easy tending and inspection of crops and the opportunity to bring different materials into the garden setting. Whether made of chunky, long-lasting railway sleepers, characterful timbers such as knotty oak and Douglas fir, or streamlined metals such as zinc and rust-brown Cor-Ten steel, your choice of raised bed will influence the character of the garden (and likewise, the character of your garden will probably influence your choice of raised bed). Preformed beds made from panels of powder-coated corrugated steel have a mid-century, retro ambience and they can be found in a nice range of colors. Alternatively, beds made from bricks in the time-honored way have undoubted solidity, permanence, and a traditional feel. A double skin of brick-work walling, with brick-on-edge coping along the top provides a satisfyingly sturdy low wall which is pleasant to sit on, perhaps with a cup of something hot, while planning future crops in situ.

Those are aesthetic considerations but, when allied to the numerous practical advantages of raised beds, it is not surprising that they are the default choice for many gardeners, especially where constantly changing food crops are concerned. Raised beds lift the surface area above that of the surrounding ground level, thereby making drainage quicker and the contained soil somewhat drier. That is an important benefit when you are spring planting after what may

→ Regular rectangular raised beds laid out in a grid pattern bring visual order to the productive garden, especially during periods of chaotic bounty, when the growing season is in full swing. Good-quality metal raised beds are generally long-lasting, and suitable in northern climates, where the daily temperatures are not too high.

well have been a long, rainy winter. Drier soil warms up more quickly too, giving early sowings and plantings a better start than they would experience at ground level. Best of all, no spadework digging is required; the trowel and hand fork become your best helpers.

You can tailor the soil in your raised bed to the optimum conditions your plants would like to grow in—not too heavy, not too light, just right. In this respect, an important practical consideration at the outset is, how high do you want the bed to be raised? The higher the bed, the more material will be required to fill it (although, only the top twelve inches or so will be used by many cropping plants, so the best soil should be reserved for the top layer). If crops such as potatoes and long carrots are intended to be grown, go for reasonable depth. Also, bear in mind that a depth of ten inches or so will be needed for securely sinking in the poles for trellis and tepees to be used by peas, climbing beans, sweet peas, tomatoes, and some cucurbits.

While deciding on your bed's ideal height is fundamental, its width is no less so. To enable comfortable tending of crops from the sidelines and avoid the need to walk on the bed, a width of about three to four feet is standard.

↑ Where a lot of produce is being grown, the paths need to be wide enough to accommodate the use of a wheelbarrow, while the raised beds can be built to whatever height you find most convenient. A well-ordered greenhouse extends both the growing season and the range of produce that can be grown.

BIO

As happens so often in gardening, we find that convenient methods and designs have been with us for many centuries. Various medieval artworks display gardens where raised beds are being cultivated. Laid out in rows and grids with access paths in between, the slender beds portrayed in woodcuts of the Middle Ages seem not at all unlike the popular designs being created and tended by us today.

← The square foot method has gained a devoted following for many years. It provides an "easy recipe" approach to growing a range of vegetables in a small space and is especially good for novice gardeners, as well as children, who enjoy being given manageable-sized squares to tend.

The Square Foot Method

Raised beds are especially well suited to a method known as "square foot gardening," which is exactly as it sounds. The surface of the designated bed is divided into square, one-foot modules, with each area outlined by a pinned down grid of canes, slender strips of wood, or just string.

The square foot method is especially good for both small gardens and novice gardeners, because an ideal starting point is a bed just four by four feet, which, when divided up, will give you sixteen individual planting areas. The inventor of the method, American former engineer and efficiency expert Mel Bartholomew, calculated the optimum number of various edibles that will grow comfortably within each square, in order to get the best productivity in a small space.

Plants are tabulated in a suggested formula: 1-4-9-16, according to how much space they need. Thus, only one plant of tomato, pepper, cabbage, kale, or cauliflower will comfortably grow in a single square, but four loose-leaf or cos lettuces can thrive in the same sized area, or sixteen radishes or carrots. Climbing beans could be between one and four, depending on variety, and nine for beets or turnips. To some degree, ideal numbering depends upon the varieties grown and whether you are keen on harvesting "baby vegetables"—such as golf ball–sized beets or miniature carrots—which could mean growing sixteen, instead of only nine.

A square-foot bed can, of course, be considerably larger than four by four, but the four-foot width is convenient for tending and harvesting from both sides. Beds four by eight feet are popular, giving thirty-two individual "cells"; four by twelve feet—not a large amount of space—potentially makes forty-eight cells available, perhaps for adding some herbs, fruits, or companion flowers to the mix.

One of the best things about square foot gardening is that it is often very appealing to children, who enjoy being given manageable-sized squares to tend. Likewise, many adults who thought they did not like gardening have been drawn in by experiencing small successes from the start, instead of being overwhelmed by attempting to manage a large, unwieldy plot of weed-prone, difficult ground. The raised, square foot bed is ideally filled with good quality potting mix, with added vermiculite that helps to maintain aeration and improve soil structure. Location is important as well, of course. Choose a bright, open situation receiving a minimum of six to eight hours of direct sunlight every day, then look forward to a constant stream of mini-harvests and mini-resowings.

→→ An ordered arrangement of tall, square beds in galvanized steel. In a tiny courtyard, it is surprising how much can be grown and easily tended from day to day.

→ A raised bed made from Cor-Ten steel nurtures a range of heirloom and heritage lettuce varieties, including: 'Marvel of Four Seasons', 'Nymans', 'Reine de Glace', 'Freckles', 'Little Gem', and modern iceberg variety 'Robinson'.

Heirloom or Modern: Which Is Best?

"Heritage'" or "heirloom" vegetables are just what their name suggests: They have withstood the test of time and are still with us. Modern F1 hybrid varieties have been bred chiefly with commercial crops in mind, with such advantages as improved disease resistance, reliably high yields, and uniform maturity, but some of these aspects are not necessarily as useful or appealing to the home gardener as, say, unique taste, an extended cropping period or, indeed, character.

Whereas the seeds of F1 hybrids need to be pollinated under strictly controlled conditions to achieve the uniformity required in agriculture, heritage vegetables have been selected across time, in the open garden or family farm, pollinated by bees and other creatures or the wind. Sometimes, people confuse F1 hybrids with genetically modified (GM) crops, but they are completely different. F1s are bred by crossing different varieties within the same species to achieve the desired effects mentioned above. GMOs are created by altering the plant's genetic makeup directly via bioengineering, introducing genetic material from completely different sources. Bt corn, for example, is a GMO that has been altered to contain genetic material from a bacterium, not a plant.

The best heirloom cultivars have been perpetuated and handed down for generations and are cherished because they have complex tastes and are suited to certain climates or soil types. Hence, their names tend to inform us of their (cultivated, not native) origins, as in the red pepper 'Corno di Toro Rosso'—long and pointed like a bull's horn—and the characterful 'Tromboncino' squash, both developed long ago in Italy. Endives such as 'Cornet d'Anjou' and 'Cornet de Bordeaux' were raised in western France; the shishito pepper hails from Japan. The juicy, sweet cherry tomato 'Gardener's Delight' has been around for at least 150 years and shows no waning in popularity, with either amateur or commercial growers.

Thousands of catalogued heirloom vegetables are grown around the world, and the adventurous cottage gardener may be tempted to try a few different ones from year to year. Finding them has been made infinitely easier via online searching and purchasing. They certainly add an interesting perspective to both garden and kitchen; it is enjoyable to compare them to the newest F1 hybrid releases, to see which works best in your environment.

↓ Raised beds made from woven hazel hurdles. Their convenient height makes an easier job of tending the contents—in this case, assorted herbs and lettuces.

→→ A well-designed, productive area: The raised beds are made from stout timbers, to be secure and long-lasting. Rows of fragrant lavender are attractive for everyone, including pollinators.

Artichokes

Cynara scolymus

A warm, sunny location protected from strong winds suits the dramatic globe artichoke, which comes from Mediterranean lands. From its core in the ground, a big plant with a lot of handsome leaves is created, out of which rise stems bearing green or purple flower heads (the "chokes") with fleshy scales. They are harvested before they open, for the delicious hearts deep inside. For edible purposes, the flowers must not be allowed to develop, but if they do, they open into magnificent purple thistles, much enjoyed by insects foraging for nectar and pollen. Where space allows, globe artichokes are handsome enough in both leaf and flower to be grown in the ornamental garden.

GROWING ARTICHOKES

Young plants are grown from seeds of named varieties or offsets (small shoots with their own roots). Artichokes enjoy light and loamy soils that are free draining but with high fertility, so preparation of the ground includes adding plenty of well-rotted manure or garden compost, ahead of spring planting. Young plants will produce a few small heads in their first year, which should be removed to encourage the plant to concentrate on becoming established. To get the best out of the plant, it needs regular watering in dry periods and an annual mulch to maintain the soil in top condition. Protect new plants from slug and snail damage, especially in wet weather.

Best Varieties
Green Globe · Gros vert de Laon
Imperial Star · Purple Globe
Romanesco · Violet de Provence

↓ Ready for harvest: Artichoke 'Purple Globe'.

→ Cut asparagus once plants are established, from year three and on.

Asparagus

Asparagus officinalis

The roots of asparagus somewhat resemble a multi-legged sea creature. Known as the "crown," the roots send up delicious, edible shoots (spears) in mid- to late spring. Asparagus is a long-term crop, requiring it to be left in situ for years on end, as it gets more settled and productive. While tradition suggests that a substantial area should allotted for the asparagus bed, it is not really necessary. Part of any bed (including raised beds) could be set aside, provided the location enjoys plenty of sunshine and shelter from cold spring winds.

GROWING ASPARAGUS

Richly fertile, well-manured soil with good drainage is essential. Crowns are spaced some eighteen inches apart and six inches deep, in rows or small groups, with the planting hole topped with enough soil to cover the outspread roots and plant tips. More soil is gradually added as the first stems grow, until the general surface level is reached. The spears must not be cut in the first two years. Patience is rewarded in year three, when spears can be harvested until early summer, after which the remaining spears need to be left to grow and develop their ferny foliage, building up strength in the plant for the following year.

Aubergines—see Eggplants

Best Varieties

Conovers Colossal · Franklin
Giant Mammoth · Jersey Giant
Lucullus · Purple Passion
Sutton's Perfection · Lorella

Beans and Peas

Phaseolus coccineus, P. vulgaris, Pisum sativum

A row of scarlet runner beans, scrambling over an A-frame of hazel poles, has been a traditional component of the cottage garden for centuries. Combining both the beauty of their fresh leaves and flowers with culinary promise via the continuously cropping pods, runner beans sit at the heart of the productive summer garden.

In their homeland of Mexico, runner beans are perennial, but they are tender, and therefore grown as annuals in cool, northern climates.

Early varieties were primarily red-flowered, but modern cultivars are available in a wider range including pink, white, salmon, and pretty two-tone kinds. Modern breeding has also created smooth-skinned pods and stringless beans that are much more pleasant to prepare and to eat.

Although the A-frame support of rustic poles is traditional and economical, the beans will grow just as decoratively over a permanent arch or trellis. They may also mix well with climbing roses, if the beans are planted at intervals between the roses on a pergola structure. For this sort of arrangement, you might want to choose a flower to fit in harmoniously among the roses, if their flowering is going to overlap. A tall, conical tepee of canes is another good method of support, especially if space is more limited. The canes should be at least eight feet long, preferably a bit more, as the first foot or so will be plunged into the ground for stability.

However they are supported, beans like a fertile, well-manured soil and a sunny location with shelter from wind. Sowing is best done under cover well into spring, so they will not be planted until after risk of frost has passed. There are also dwarf varieties that suit being grown in patio pots.

French beans, or haricots verts, come in both climbing varieties (grown the same way as runners) and as dwarf bushes. Both are very prolific, with tasty, easily harvested pods. Sowing at four-week intervals until mid-July will bring a succession of harvests of tender young beans. 'Borlotto Lingua Di Fuoco' (tongue of fire), also known as the cranberry or borlotti bean, is a glamorous heirloom bush variety with crimson streaks. When very young and tender, they can be cooked and eaten whole, like runner beans, but the mature, shelled beans are more versatile.

Likewise, the broad bean, or fava (*Vicia faba*). Varieties with reasonable frost tolerance can be planted in autumn for harvesting in late spring/early summer (for example, 'Super Aquadulce', 'Aquadulce Claudia', and 'Luz de Otono'). If you live in a cold area, leave planting until late spring. Broad beans are attractive in both leaf and flower and waft a delicate scent that draws the bumble- and honeybees to pollinate. For something a bit different from the black-and-white blooms, try 'Crimson Flowered', a heritage variety from the eighteenth century. Achieving just three feet (90 cm) or so, it is decorative and compact enough to grow in medium-sized containers. Even more compact is 'The Sutton'. Achieving some twelve to eighteen inches but cropping well, it is the perfect pint-sized pod plant for productive patio pots.

Peas require adequate support, so prepare a network of pea sticks (cut from twiggy, bare branches in winter), a willow fence, or trellis for their tendrils to cling to from the start. Where space or time is limited, I would concentrate on the mange-tout and sugar snap varieties. They tend to yield larger crops for the space, are delicious, and save time since you eat the whole pod and don't need to spend time shelling.

'Oregon Sugar Pod' and 'Growmax' yield well with sweet, crunchy pods. 'Purple Magnolia' resembles a decorative sweet pea, climbing some six to eight feet tall with lots of two-tone pink-and-red flowers followed by dark purple sugar snaps. The equally decorative 'Blauwschokker' (Dutch for blue pod) is a handsome heritage pea whose dark pods can be harvested early as snap peas.

Being legumes, beans and peas play an invaluable role in the garden's soil, drawing atmospheric nitrogen into nodules on their roots. When cropping is over, just cutting the stems back to ground level and leaving the roots to decompose enriches the soil for a future crop. For this reason, leafy brassicas such as kales and their kin especially benefit from the natural nitrogen left behind in the earth, if planted where the legumes previously grew.

← Scarlet runner beans, an old cottage garden staple.

→→ Peas galore, among woven willow, including the deep pink-and-white heirloom 'Crown Pea'.

Beets and Chards

Beta vulgaris

Beets (or beetroots, globe beets) and chards (also known as Swiss chards, or leaf beet) are among the easiest and most reliable of home-grown crops—and some of the most colorful. They are all descended from the wild green sea beet inhabiting coastlines of numerous countries around the world. Long ago found to be palatable, sea beets were variously cultivated and refined: in one direction for better, fleshier leaves, and in the opposite direction for larger roots. The leaves were popular in the ancient world (Aristotle noted red-stemmed chards), and the Romans developed swollen-rooted red beets. Appreciated for their earthy sweetness, beetroots were still referred to as "Roman beets" in the late Middle Ages.

Sow seed in small batches from spring to midsummer, to get a succession of harvests from early summer to mid-autumn. When densely planted they will grow quite quickly into a convenient golf ball size, with tender flesh that cooks quickly. Beets are versatile for pickling, chopping, or roasting with olive oil and herbs. I like to grow two or three varieties to serve up an eye-catching plate of different shades of beet carpaccio, finely sliced, with some little leaves of watercress or arugula and a mild Gorgonzola or Dolcelatte cheese.

Some seed companies sell 'Rainbow Mixed' beet collections, with red, white, yellow, and 'Chioggia' types, the latter having concentric rosy-red and white rings all the way through. 'Bull's Blood' is popular for its dark crimson young leaves to put in "baby leaf" salads, as well as for its roots. 'Burpee's Golden' has superb, bright yellow flesh in the roots, contained within an orange skin. Grow beets in a bright, open location in light, well broken, and fertile soil.

↓ 'Rainbow Mixed' beets.

↑ 'Bright Lights' chards.

With its shiny, deeply crumpled leaf blades and contrasting brightly hued stems, Swiss chard is handsome enough to grow among garden ornamentals. It also makes a splendid temporary potted plant, provided the container is deep enough for the long taproot it will send down to anchor the substantial foliage (a pot at least twelve inches deep is good). Sow direct in mid- to late spring. If you are preparing a raised bed for a row of chard, most aspects suit it well, including somewhere partially shaded for a few hours each day. A bit of shade can be an advantage in hot summers—not so much in a dull and overcast season. The soil should be fertile and well-manured to be moisture-retentive, since those large leaves will draw up a lot of water when in full sail.

The variety 'Fordhook Giant' is among the hardiest, with broad, white ribs. 'Bright Lights' is superb and uplifting, thanks to the seed mixture's variety of reds, pinks, oranges, yellows, and white stems. It can be grown year-round but is less frost hardy than other chards. 'Giallo', with yellow ribs, and 'Rhubarb' or 'Ruby' chard, with red ribs, both make vibrant, attractive for salads, before the plant matures.

Cabbages and Kales

Brassica oleracea, B. o. var. acephala, and others

Hardy, leafy, nutritious, and often delicious, brassicas are the ultimate cottage garden plants, which fed the medieval cottars when there was not much else available to them.

Collectively, brassicas also contributed to ancient herbal remedies, such as easing gout, cleansing ulcers, and sharpening sight. A "smoothie" of juiced kale or cabbage was known even in the times of the ancient Greeks and Romans as a cure for a hangover. (We now understand why: It was replacing electrolytes and vitamins depleted by alcohol. Truly, there is nothing new under the sun!)

The cabbages, kales, kohlrabies, cauliflowers, Brussels sprouts, and broccolis so familiar to us (but so different from each other) are all the results of the species' naturally promiscuous gene exchange. Their willingness to hybridize means that people continue to develop interesting new crosses, just as they did long ago, in the days of Theophrastus and Pliny. Kalettes, or "flower sprouts," for example, are modern F1 hybrids that were painstakingly developed over some fifteen years by selective hybridizing (not genetic modification). They reveal the attributes of their parents in an interesting way, combining the diminutive size and stalked arrangement of Brussels sprouts with the curly foliage seen in some kales. The results are novelty, miniature "rosettes" with very frilly leaves: slow to grow but quick to cook, and small enough to stir-fry whole.

Oriental brassicas (selections of *B. rapa*) are as diverse as their European counterparts and well worth including in the productive garden. I especially like the Chinese cabbage, *B. rapa* subsp. *pekinensis*, with its tightly packed, pale heads of wrapped-over leaves, so sweet and crunchy in salads, but just as good steamed or stir-fried. Mizuna, *B. rapa* var. *japonica*, has peppery, deeply cut leaves, and probably originated in China but has been cultivated in Japan since antiquity. In the modern cottage garden, they can be tucked in almost anywhere, especially in pots and window boxes, for cut-and-come-again salad leaves.

Leafy brassicas are easy to grow if attention is paid to their specific needs. They love deep, fertile soils with a neutral to high pH, so if your soil is below 7, add some lime or calcified seaweed to neutralize any acidity. In typical northern European conditions, they need a bright, open, and wind-sheltered position, but in warm climates, partial afternoon shade is desirable. Rotate the crops from year to year, so that common diseases do not get established in the soil. Brassicas are hungry feeders, with high nitrogen requirements to establish good leaf growth. Added seaweed fertilizer contributes valuable magnesium and trace minerals for allover plant health. All brassicas are attractive to pests, especially pigeons, slugs, and caterpillars, so use physical barriers such as row covers or netting where required. Companion plants such as sacrificial nasturtiums attract some insect pests away from your crops, while the strong scent of nearby mint can help deflect flea beetles.

↑ Deeply cut leaves of mizuna.

→ Broccoli, red cabbage, and 'Cavolo Nero' kale.

SOME BRASSICAS TO TRY

Cabbage 'Charleston Wakefield'
suits warm areas; a heat-tolerant, pointed head heirloom variety

Cabbage 'Greyhound'
neat and compact, fast-growing pointed cabbage

Cabbage 'January King'
an impressive heirloom classic; very hardy with green and purple slightly crinkled leaves

Cabbage 'Mammoth Red Rock'
delicious and reliable heirloom red cabbage

Cabbage 'Stelvio F1'
a pointed Savoy type with neat heads and attractive crinkled leaves

Chinese cabbage 'Pak Choi Red'
bright green and purple loose-leaved cabbage for baby leaf salads, or matured for stir-frys

Chinese cabbage 'Scarvita F1'
unusual, crimson-purple variety; brightens up a salad

Chinese cabbage 'Yuki F1'
classic, crunchy hearts and good disease resistance

Kale 'Buttonhole Starmaker'
flamboyant rosettes with bright pink heart and veins

Kale 'Cavolo Nero'
versatile Tuscan kale with long, very dark, crinkled leaves

Kale 'Dwarf Green Curled'
compact, frizzy-leaved heritage variety suitable for pots

Kale 'Red Russian'
very popular and very hardy; fast-growing with incised, pink-veined leaves

Kale 'Taunton Deane'
a very old, hardy perennial kale; nonflowering but sold as cuttings and potted plants

Kale 'Yurok F1'
a compact, Cavolo Nero type suitable for containers

Kalettes 'Garden Mix F1'
tasty and slender, good for containers and raised beds

Carrots

Daucus carota

Easy to grow in successional sowings for a long season of harvests, carrots count as one of the best vegetables to grow at home. While they come in a rainbow spectrum from deep purples and reds through orange and yellow to creamy-white, it is the familiar, cheerful orange that prevails in most cultivars.

Most carrots grow best in light but fertile soils of neutral to slightly acidic pH. A sandy loam enriched with old, well-rotted manure or compost and without obstructive stones is ideal and, of course, growing carrots in a raised bed can provide such conditions if the natural ground is very different. Seeds are sown thinly about half-an-inch deep, to be thinned out later, and will need some cover protection with cloches or fleece to protect from cold weather and seasonal pests such as carrot fly, if the pests are a problem locally.

There are countless varieties, some of which have especially useful characteristics. The F1 hybrids 'Fly Away', 'Maestro', and 'Resistafly', for example, were selectively bred to have inherent resistance to carrot root fly; they do not have complete immunity but are less attractive to the pest. The heritage variety 'Danvers' has a strong constitution and copes with heavy soils better than most others, resisting splitting in compacted ground.

Arguably, the best tasting carrot, if you were only going to grow one, is the French heritage variety 'Early Nantes'. The chef Raymond Blanc, who has carried out extensive taste tests for decades in the gardens of Le Manoir aux Quat'Saisons, in Oxfordshire, is a lifelong fan.

Carrots grow well in containers—even window boxes—and one just has to choose varieties suited to the depth of soil available. Short, or "dumpy" carrots, such as 'Paris Market Round' (also known as 'Tonda di Parigi') are fast maturing and immensely popular for pot and window box gardening, being ready for harvest when the spherical roots are golf ball size. This cherished French heirloom has been grown since the nineteenth century.

SOME CARROTS TO TRY

White
Blanche a Collet Vert
Crème de Lite
Lunar White
White Satin

Yellow
Amarillo
Gold Nugget
Jaune Obtuse de Doubs
Yellow Moon

Red and Purple
Atomic Red
Cosmic Purple
Purple Haze
Rouge Sang Violette

Orange
Bolero
Caracas (short)
Chantenay Red Cored (short)
De Luc
Danvers
Early Nantes
Imperator
Little Finger (short)
Paris Market Round (short)

→ Not just orange: A harvest of multihued carrots.

Eggplants or Aubergines

Solanum melongena

Aubergines, or eggplants, are tender perennials of tropical Asia and, given a warm or hot season, will perform well, producing purple, pinky-lilac, or white flowers (depending on the variety) followed by many shiny fruits among large, felty leaves.

When summers turn out to be cold and damp (which aubergines often are in the British Isles), they are best grown in the greenhouse, alongside tomatoes, to which they are related. Since they make excellent subjects for growing in pots, you can have the best of both worlds, raising them in nutrient-rich potting compost under glass and, if summer provides plenty of sunshine and real warmth, they can go outside and perform decoratively and productively. Some skins are marbled, speckled, or striped, especially in the crimson/white range; once they get going, the fruits grow quite rapidly and quantities across the season may be plentiful.

While on their own these spongy fruits are bland and not especially remarkable, when chopped and cooked, they readily absorb the oils and spices in dishes such as curries and sauces. In European cooking, they are an iconic ingredient of French ratatouille, Greek moussaka, and in traditional dishes of southern Spain, where summer's heat ensures bountiful crops.

Apart from the sunshine and shelter requirement, these plants need regular feeding and watering when producing fruit and tying to canes as they grow. If insects are scarce and pollination is not naturally occurring, tickling all the flowers with a small paintbrush will suffice.

→ Stripey 'Listada de Gandia'.

↓ Curvaceous and cheerful: Dark purple 'Zora', a mostly white 'Rosa Bianca', and curly 'Farmer's Long'.

Onions and Garlic

Allium cepa, Allium sativum

"You have to respect an onion," says chef Raymond Blanc. "It is a powerful weapon of flavor, but it has to be tamed through cooking, because it is full of substances that can make you cry and give you flatulence." Blanc, the continuous holder of two Michelin stars for more than three decades, and the proprietor of an experimental organic kitchen garden second to none (at Le Manoir aux Quat'Saisons in Oxfordshire), is always worth listening to regarding the most worthwhile edibles to grow.

For general cooking, Blanc likes a white onion, such as the Scottish heritage variety 'Ailsa Craig', which is sweet in character and caramelizes well. For delivering onion "character" and depth, perhaps in an onion soup, his preferred variety is 'Rose de Roscoff', also known as 'Keravel Pink'. This attractive, centuries-old heirloom onion has an interesting story. From about 1828 onward, French growers from the coast of Brittany packed their onions and made the shortish sea crossing to the British Isles to sell them. Except during wartime, the established trade lasted nearly two hundred years. I remember seeing the Breton sellers and their bicycles burdened with many plaits of onions and garlics, calling door-to-door in summer and autumn. Sadly, various insurmountable challenges in the twenty-first century have wiped out this charming traditional trade.

In the onion tribe, my own preference is for banana shallots, so named for their elongated shape; they are also known as *echalions*. They are milder and sweeter than the pungent, eye-watering onions more widely grown and are very easy to peel and slice. The varieties 'Zebrune', 'Longor', and 'Simiane' are all excellent and versatile.

Onions usually make easy and reliable plants. They need a sunny, open location and well-drained soil that was manured or composted in autumn. Seed-sowings can be made from late winter into spring, but growing from sets (baby onions) in mid-spring saves time, and they develop sooner (but will likely need bird protection early on). In areas prone to wet weather, look for mildew-resistant varieties such as 'Bonus F1', 'Santero F1', and 'Redlander'.

Garlic (*Allium sativum*) is grown by planting individual cloves in light soil some two inches deep and six inches apart, in a sunny location. Plantings from autumn to early spring will yield harvests from early to high summer; a touch of cold in the winter helps the plant form a good bulb. 'Extra Early Wight' is one of a number of renowned British varieties from the Isle of Wight, hardy with clean white bulbs. 'Rose Wight' and 'Chesnok Red' are beautiful varieties with purple pinstripes.

Courgettes—see Zucchinis

← Onions 'Ailsa Craig' with lettuce 'Little Red Gem'.

→ Kitchen garden harvest, with garlic 'Solent White'.

Peppers and Chiles

Capsicum annuum and C. baccatum

Like tomatoes, peppers are rewarding to grow, because they are generous with their fruits and, once fruiting is underway, you can see progress virtually from day to day, as they grow and ripen. The level of "reward" comes with a caveat, however. These are plants that must have adequate warmth and sunshine to develop satisfactorily.

Chiles and sweet peppers are all cultivated the same way. The original species are native to South America, and several species were consumed in the Americas for thousands of years.

For the gardener and the cook, a large part of the attraction of peppers is their very wide range of sizes, colors, and heat. There are boxy shapes; long, pointed peppers; triangular, round, and curled. They run through the spectrum from green to yellow to orange, red, purple, and black. The heat scale depends on the level of the chemical compound capsaicin present in each variety. The capsaicin or Scoville scale measures heat from zero, as in sweet bell peppers with no heat, to a blistering more than two million Scoville Heat Units (SHU); hot habaneros and Scotch bonnet achieve between 100,000 and 350,000. One of the hottest of the more recent "super hot" varieties bears the somewhat tongue-in-cheek name 'Armageddon'. I will leave that one for someone else to enjoy. Being mostly compact plants that enjoy pot cultivation, chiles are a great choice for growing on patios, windowsills, or even indoors in the sunniest spot. It is advisable to wear gloves when harvesting them.

↓ Medium-hot 'Hungarian Hot Wax' chiles with companion plants of French marigolds and basil.

→ Slender heirloom variety 'Joe's Long Cayenne'.

Peppers need a long season with masses of sunshine to reliably mature, which is by no means certain in temperate climates such as northern Europe's. For this reason, growing peppers under the extra protection of a greenhouse improves the chances of getting ripened fruits. Even in a greenhouse, peppers can struggle in an overcast, rainy summer and may require help from an electric "grow light" that delivers the full spectrum of sunlight for seven or eight hours per day.

Peppers are extremely amenable to being grown in a pot and for most gardeners, this is the best method. For those who do not want to grow from seed, young plants of many varieties are sold online and in garden stores these days. Use a freely draining potting compost with some added perlite or vermiculite for extra aeration and drainage and repot plants periodically, as required. Feed and water established plants regularly. A big, final pot (of some twenty liters/ five US gallons) is helpful to enable root access to enough feed and water, producing a stronger, more productive plant.

When growing under glass, peppers are often targeted by whiteflies and aphids, so they need checking regularly. The best deterrent companion plants to grow among them are French marigolds (*Tagetes patula*), pot marigolds (*Calendula officinalis*), and also basil, which is not only a good repellent, it also enhances the taste of the peppers.

RECOMMENDED SWEET PEPPERS

California Wonder
classic and versatile heirloom bell pepper; large, sweet fruits, matures from green to red

Cardinal
bell type; very mild and sweet, ripening stages dark purple to red

Corno di Toro Rosso
sweet, long and tapering "bull's horn" fruits, ripening early, red

Liberty Belle F1
forms compact plants well suited to patio pots; high yield of versatile, sweet fruits, matures deep yellow

Marconi Rossa
late nineteenth-century heirloom; crops well with very sweet, elongated red fruits

Mohawk
compact and semitrailing, suited to patio pots and hanging baskets, with abundant small fruits, maturing green to orange

New Ace F1
extra early and very productive; ripens green to red

Pusztagold
very sweet, Hungarian variety; early ripening, yellow to red

Snackbite
Mini sweet peppers on small plant (twenty to twenty-four inches); orange to red

RECOMMENDED CHILE PEPPERS

Anaheim
Long peppers also known as New Mexico or Magdalena pepper; versatile in dishes, due to low to medium heat

Apache F1
Popular, compact and prolific; medium-hot chiles, green to red

Cayenne
long, thin, red chiles with intense heat; widely grown and popular dried and ground into powder

Friar's Hat
also known as Bishop's Crown, with hat- or flange-shaped fruits; decorative, scarlet fruits with mild to medium heat

Habanero
closely related to Scotch bonnet; blazing hot chiles, lantern-shaped; various subdivided habanero varieties include 'Chocolate', 'Orange', 'The Monster', and 'Fruit Burst'—all very hot

Lemon Drop
hot, with bright yellow fruits and lemony, citrus notes

Ring of Fire
very thin fruits, very early cropping and very hot indeed

Potatoes

Solanum tuberosum

Baked, mashed, boiled, fried, roasted, waffled, sautéed with bacon, sliced for a dauphinoise, or chopped for a chowder, the humble potato is one of the most delicious and versatile edibles to cook, as well as to cultivate.

Potatoes are often planted into fresh ground, where they help prepare the way for subsequent crops, since their deep root systems loosen the soil by creating pockets of air and improving its structure. They do not need extensive areas in order to grow, unless there is a requirement for a large amount, especially for winter storage. When growing potatoes for storage, choose main crop varieties that mature nicely over a long season and will grow to a substantial size. Early, or "new" potatoes, are grown for a quicker turnaround, being generally smaller than main crops and having a waxy, firm texture, thin skins, and delicate taste, perfectly accompanied by butter.

Sprouting or "chitting" seed potatoes some six weeks before planting encourages new shoots to emerge. Place them somewhere light, standing in a box (egg cartons can be good for this) with the end that has the most "eyes" facing upward. Early varieties may be planted in early to mid-spring, but frost is the potato's enemy, so protect with cloches and straw if necessary, or plant a bit later in cold areas. Main crop varieties follow in mid- to late spring, depending on local conditions. Potatoes grown in raised beds and containers do not require "earthing up," but it is often done for plants in the ground, by using a hoe to pile up some earth or compost around the growing stem to help keep light away from the developing tubers beneath the surface. Earlies are ready to harvest some twelve to fifteen weeks after planting, or when the flowers are fully out. Main crops can carry on until the leaves go brown in autumn, when the top growth can be cut back. Leaving the crop in the ground for another couple of weeks helps a thicker, stronger skin develop, which is needed for successful storage.

POPULAR POTATO VARIETIES

Early or "New" Potatoes

Arran Pilot
Belle de Fontenay
Charlotte*
Jazzy*
La Ratte*
Pentland Javelin
Red Duke of York
Swift

**Second early: summer crops, planted in late spring and developing quickly, twelve to fifteen weeks after planting.*

Main Crop

Albert Bartlett Rooster
Desiree
Excelsior
King Edward
Maris Piper
Mayan Rose
Russet
Yukon Gold

← Healthy young potato plants in a well-planned raised bed.

→ Harvesting 'Wilja', a versatile, second early variety for summer crops.

Pumpkins and Winter Squash

Cucurbita maxima, Cucurbita moschata

Pumpkins and squashes dramatically see off the summer. Their culinary comforts are impressive and welcome when daylight hours are shrinking and cold weather rolls in.

The (frequently orange) flesh contained under their hard skins seems endlessly adaptable to baking, roasting, and making soup. Pumpkins and their kin fill out pies, tarts, gratins, flans, frittatas, and vegetable bakes. These wonderful vegetables (which technically are fruits) pair well with bacon, various continental charcuteries, and old-fashioned English black pudding. They may be subtly enhanced by spices such as cinnamon, cardamom, nutmeg, star anise, pepper, or paprika. A soup made of pumpkin and pears, or butternut and golden beetroot, or simple squash and sage is dependably warming and satisfying.

The Americas have introduced many culinary treasures to the world, and the cucurbits are right up there among the best of them.

The difference between summer squashes (p. 232) and winter squashes is that the summer kinds have thin skins and need to be eaten fresh. Their storage life is very short, unless they are dried or frozen. Winter squashes have a protective, hard rind, which, undamaged, enables simple storage for several months.

Winter squashes have much the same cultivation requirements as their summer cousins. They are hungry, thirsty plants that need a very fertile, well-manured soil; it is no accident that these plants are regularly grown on the top of mature compost heaps; the long-established practice enables direct access to all the nutrients the plant requires. In other situations, a fortnightly sprinkling of chicken manure pellets and a drench with seaweed liquid feed will do just fine. Choose a bright, open, sunny location; surrounding the plants with a weed-suppressing membrane or mulch is a time-saver in a spacious pumpkin patch. Where space is more limited, grow butternuts and the smaller-sized pumpkins vertically, on an arch, a secure trellis, or a meshed, metal tunnel. Harvest ripe plants before they get too big or hit by frosts, leaving a tail attached to the fruit, on each stem.

↑ Nothing says autumn quite so vividly as the squash and pumpkin harvest.

→ A traditional pumpkin patch, with Hokkaido Squash 'Uchiki Kuri', 'Black Futsu', and French heirloom 'Galeux d'Eysines', also known as 'Peanut Pumpkin' or 'Warted Sugar Marrow'.

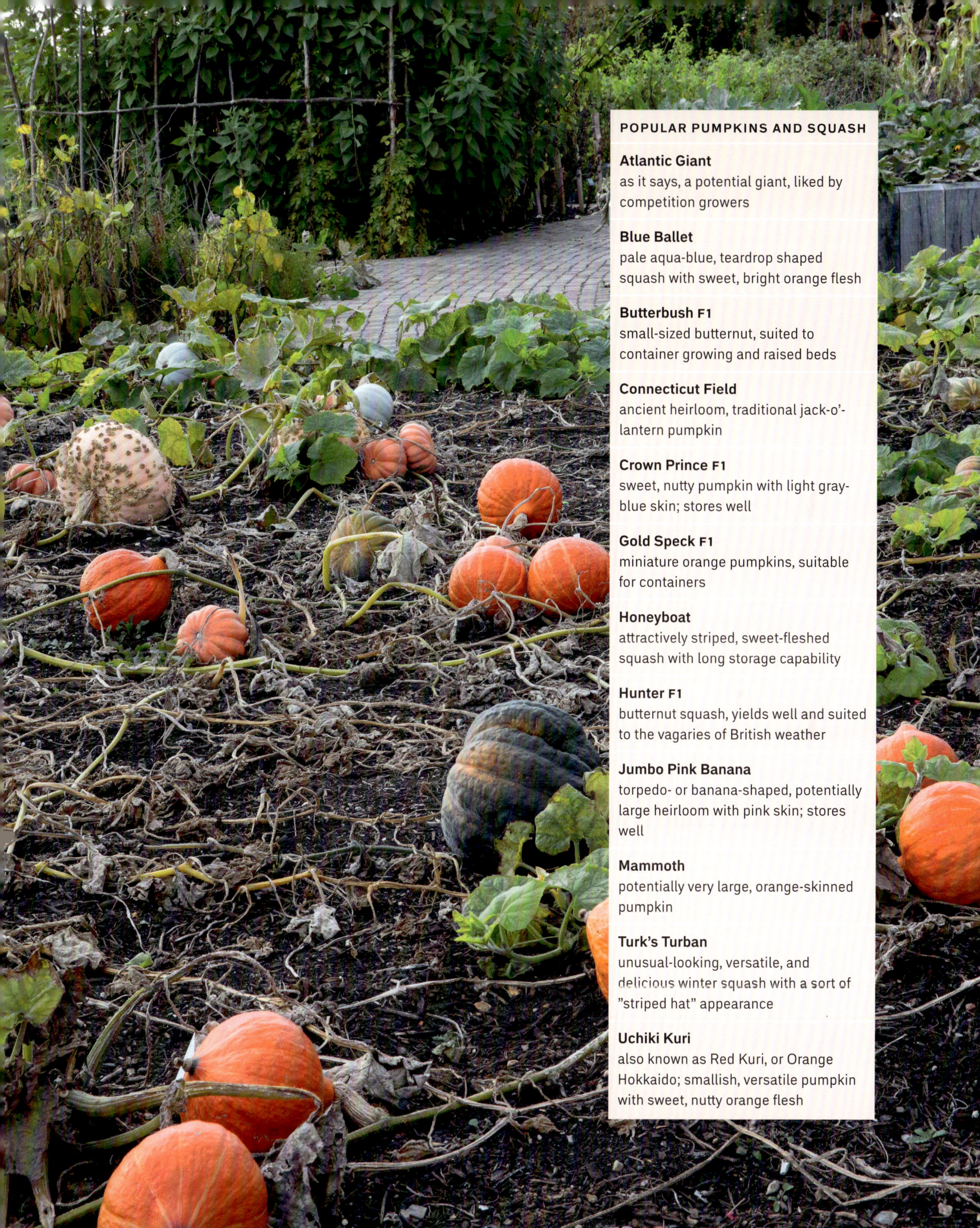

POPULAR PUMPKINS AND SQUASH

Atlantic Giant
as it says, a potential giant, liked by competition growers

Blue Ballet
pale aqua-blue, teardrop shaped squash with sweet, bright orange flesh

Butterbush F1
small-sized butternut, suited to container growing and raised beds

Connecticut Field
ancient heirloom, traditional jack-o'-lantern pumpkin

Crown Prince F1
sweet, nutty pumpkin with light gray-blue skin; stores well

Gold Speck F1
miniature orange pumpkins, suitable for containers

Honeyboat
attractively striped, sweet-fleshed squash with long storage capability

Hunter F1
butternut squash, yields well and suited to the vagaries of British weather

Jumbo Pink Banana
torpedo- or banana-shaped, potentially large heirloom with pink skin; stores well

Mammoth
potentially very large, orange-skinned pumpkin

Turk's Turban
unusual-looking, versatile, and delicious winter squash with a sort of "striped hat" appearance

Uchiki Kuri
also known as Red Kuri, or Orange Hokkaido; smallish, versatile pumpkin with sweet, nutty orange flesh

Sweetcorn

Zea mays

An advantage of having sweetcorn growing in the garden is that ripe cobs can be plucked from the plant and cooked straight away, since the taste and sweetness can start to fade soon after picking. Indeed, connoisseurs recommend you have a pan of boiling water sitting ready for the moment the cobs are picked and brought indoors.

Sweetcorn is a tender, annual grass and it grows best in areas experiencing long, hot summers. It is not always a successful crop in cooler northern climates with inclement seasons, but a number of modern hybrids have been bred to mature rapidly for locations where the growing and ripening period is brief. Among them, Earlibird F1 is a "super-sweet" variety; Swift F1 is as rapid as its name suggests and Northern Extra Sweet F1 is very early maturing with long, sweet cobs.

Popular heritage and heirloom varieties abound, including Early Golden Bantam and Dolce, both fast growing and delicious; Fiesta has a traditional, multihued cob and Stowell's Evergreen, a cherished nineteenth-century heirloom, is still admired by many for its sweetness and complex character.

Keen corn growers may opt for planting several strains that are ready at different times. By choosing early, mid-season, and late-ripening hybrids it is possible to harvest over a long period. Each variety needs to be grown in its own separate patch, however, to maintain the integrity of its characteristics. Sweetcorns are wind-pollinated and promiscuous, so any chance of hybrids cross-pollinating needs to be avoided. Likewise, because of wind-pollination, the seeds or young plants are set out in blocks, not lines, to make the fertilization process more successful.

In warm areas, seeds can be sown directly into the patch where they are to grow, but locations with late frosts and cold nights are better served by starting off the seeds in pots indoors and planting when all risk of cold weather has passed. Fertile, light soil with plenty of well-rotted manure mixed in suits these hungry grasses, which also need regular watering and feeding through the season.

→ Flowering time for Sweetcorn 'Conqueror'.

↓ The corn harvest hanging up to dry.

← Heirloom tomato 'Datterini Yellow' fruits prolifically.

→ Distinctively ribbed heirloom, 'Costoluto Fiorentino'.

Tomatoes

Solanum lycopersicum

Sweet, spicy, juicy, and aromatic, the ripened tomato plucked straight from the vine and eaten at once is one of the pleasures of summer in the garden. Growing tomatoes successfully is extraordinarily easy, provided you choose the right plant for the right place; therefore, some procedures are helpful in order to home in on the varieties best suited to your needs.

Tomatoes are tender perennials, usually grown as annuals and some are best grown under glass, particularly in cool regions where they can enjoy a long season, sheltered from cold winds. Many, however, are fast sprinters that can grow and fruit rapidly during a good summer outdoors, often cropping into early autumn, whether grown in beds or in some form of container. Your own location will dictate whether outdoor growing is feasible, or if the tomato experience will be more rewarding within a greenhouse or conservatory.

There are basically two growth types to choose from: tall varieties are known as "indeterminate"; unpruned, they can potentially grow several yards high and wide. Alternatively, bush or dwarf kinds are "determinate," having a predetermined size built in (between about twelve inches and four to five feet, depending on the variety). Determinate kinds are ideal for growing in patio pots and small spaces such as balconies; the absolute smallest are good candidates for growing and fruiting even in hanging baskets and window boxes.

Within the two main categories of determinate or indeterminate, they span the spectrum from light yellows and greens to the classic red and even almost black purple. There is a broad range of fruit sizes, from the smallest cherry tomatoes to "plum" shapes (popular for sauces and canning) and large beefsteak varieties, very decorative when sliced through horizontally for filling sandwiches and burgers or making beautiful salads.

Whether raised in pots, tomato grow-bags, raised beds, or in the open ground, tomatoes need a bright, sheltered location and all except the smallest need a framework of support. Indeterminate (tall) varieties are traditionally grown as cordons, up a strong, single stake, with the side shoots pinched out when they appear, to maintain order and encourage bountiful crops all the way up the stake. They can also be grown against the support of tall tepees, with several shoots retained and tied into the tepee canes. Cane or obelisk structures are good for the more vigorous of the determinate (short) varieties that might reach some four to five feet high. Compact "tumbling" tomatoes have a trailing habit and produce many cherry-sized tomatoes, cascading attractively from the sides of pots and window boxes.

Tomatoes are thirsty and hungry plants, requiring frequent watering and feeding. Harvest regularly to encourage more flowering and fruiting and routinely check for pests that damage the fruits, such as caterpillars and slugs.

SOME TOMATO VARIETIES AND THEIR USES

For Salads

Little cherry tomatoes and large beefsteaks, with some in-betweens

Black Opal
Costoluto Fiorentino
Gardener's Delight
Loveheart
Rubylicious
Supermarmande
Tigerella
Yellow Pear

For Salsas

Big Boy
Big Rainbow
Blue Ridge Mountain
Eva's Purple Ball
Golden Sunrise
Maskotka
Moneymaker
Mule Team

For Sauces and Soups

Cornue des Andes
Jersey Giant
Juliet
Long Tom
Loveheart
Olivade
Supermarmande
San Marzano Lungo

← Dark green, near-spherical 'Eight Ball'.

→ High yielding 'Gold Rush' fruits early.

Zucchinis or Courgettes

Cucurbita pepo

Part of the estimable squash family, courgettes, or zucchini, are summer squashes and among the most rewarding of vegetables, being easy, rapid growers and highly productive. Once they get going, the fruits are yielded all summer long, providing versatile food for roasting, frying, or grilling, and creating soups, stews, and ratatouille-type mixed vegetable dishes.

They are in fact actually baby marrows that taste best and are most tender when harvested small. They also come in great variety, including ball-shaped, star-shaped, and pear-shaped as well as the standard straight zucchini. Pattypan courgettes (also called summer squash) have a flattened, "flying saucer" appearance, with a scalloped edge. These very attractive fruits can be roasted whole or sliced across the wide section, to maintain the star pattern. The plants are small enough to be easily grown in patio containers and make an attractive novelty, especially enjoyed by children.

As well as assorted shapes, they come in deep yellow, pale yellow, various shades of green, and a near-white in the Italian heritage variety 'Lungo Bianco'. It is tempting to try to grow them all.

As tender annuals, they are best sown indoors or under glass from mid-spring well into summer; the young plants can go outside once there is no risk of cold weather or night chills. These are really hungry and thirsty plants and grow best in a richly manured compost. When fruiting is underway, regular attention to watering is essential as well as applications of liquid tomato feed. The first flowers are usually male, but the productive female flowers follow on regularly, thereafter.

Providing a tepee of canes or a trellis is helpful, so they can be lifted up and tied in as they grow. This enables ventilation around the stems to discourage powdery mildew, a very common problem with courgettes, which gets worse as the plants age. If you see it taking hold, prepare a milk spray—about 30 percent cow's milk mixed with 70 percent water—to spray on both sides of the leaves to slow down the attack and cut off badly affected foliage.

RECOMMENDED VARIETIES

Green
All Green Bush
Ambassador
Early Gem
Eight Ball
Firenze
Tondo di Piacenza

Pale Green/Cream
Bianca di Trieste
Ismalia
Lungo Bianco
Tromboncino

Yellow
Butterstick
Floridor
Golden Griller
Gold Rush
Lemon
Orelia

Pattypan and Scalloped
Early White Bush Scallop
Early Yellow
Scallopini
Green Disc

16 · Salads and Herbs

HERBS CAN BE ADDICTIVE. BY WHICH I MEAN THAT THE MORE YOU learn about them, the more interesting and absorbing they become. The growing of herbs goes back into the mists of time; nobody knows for how many thousands of years, but in ancient Mesopotamia, the Sumerians documented their use of herbs on clay tablets. The Egyptians recorded more than 850 herbal medicines on papyri, and in ancient Greece, numerous herbs were widely used and cultivated for culinary, medicinal, and religious purposes.

They include, of course, the familiar, aromatic Mediterranean species that have long been subsumed into Western therapeutics and/or cuisine—such as rosemary, thyme, oregano, sage, fennel, parsley, bay laurel, and saffron (*Crocus sativus*). To walk in the sunbaked hills and islands of Greece and follow the stony goat and sheep paths through its gorges is a chance to savor, at source and underfoot, the sort of herbal aromas that lure customers at mealtimes to the taverna and the pizzeria.

These same herbs were brought to the British Isles by the Romans some two thousand years ago. After they left, it was largely down to the closed communities of monasteries to preserve knowledge of herbs, grown more for medicinal purposes than culinary.

In medieval and Tudor times, aromatic herbs were used for "strewing." That is to say, the cut stalks, with the leaves and/or flowers, were scattered over floors to be trodden on, thereby masking unpleasant odors, since home interiors across the social scale tended to be shared with rodents and insect critters of various kinds. Thomas Tusser's *Five Hundred Good Points of Husbandry* (1573), noted that the best strewing herbs were, among others: basil, lemon balm, chamomile, costmary, cowslips, sweet fennel, germander, hyssop, lavender, marjoram, pennyroyal, rose petals, mint, sage, tansy, violets, and winter savory. Pennyroyal (*Mentha pulegium*)—pungently minty when crushed—was valued as a flea and tick repellent, no doubt very useful at the time.

In royal residences, an official herb strewer was engaged to distribute such herbs through the royal apartments, to obscure bad scents with more appealing, herbal fragrances. Therefore, one of the important roles of Tudor herb gardens

← Metal cauldrons have been recycled to create a delightful herb garden for thyme, lavender, rosemary, sage, basil, and lavender. The cauldrons are deep enough for small herbs, with drainage holes drilled in the bottom.

of the well-to-do was to produce strewing herbs. Most of the typical species are not difficult to propagate and steadily found their way into cottage gardens, among more mundane species.

There are various ways to grow herbs, either formally or informally, depending on your style. Most herbs can be very successfully grown in pots and, with several grouped together, a very worthwhile herb garden can be plundered for fresh material year-round. Formal herb gardens always have special allure. I recall a small, sunny courtyard garden designed by herb specialist Jekka McVicar which displayed a collection of different low-growing thymes, where the varying flower shades resonate with the gentle pink and blue tones inherent in the natural clay bricks used for the surrounding path.

A larger, sunny area with freely draining soil would be ideal for a casual, Mediterranean-inspired "garigue" gravel garden of herbs that wafts wonderful aromas in warm weather. Sage, thyme, rosemary, marjoram, lavender, and cotton lavender (*Santolina* spp.) all sit very well together, planted in loose drifts of three to five plants of each kind. Among them, small bulbs may be planted in little groups to pop up in spring, such as species tulips, narcissi, and muscari. Because the emphasis is on shrubby herbs, this type of planting is relatively low-maintenance, just needing the plants to be trimmed once or twice a year, so they do not flop and lose shape.

→ From a practical point of view, it is useful to grow culinary herbs near each other and, perhaps, not too far from the kitchen door. There is nothing to equal fresh herbs from the garden.

CLOCKWISE FROM TOP LEFT
— Golden marjoram, *Origanum vulgare* 'Aureum'
— Purple sage, *Salvia officinalis* 'Purpurascens'
— *Angelica archangelica*, with chives and borage
— Common fennel, *Foeniculum vulgare*
— Curled parsley, *Petroselinum crispum*
— A small collection of different thymes

Common fennel (*Foeniculum vulgare*) is lovely for introducing delicate, filigree fronds into sunny herbal plantings as well as height, from the five to six foot (150–80 cm) flower stems. Think ahead, though, as to how you will manage its generous production of seeds. The seeds can be harvested as soon as ripe for use in the kitchen. They can be left in situ, for birds such as finches and sparrows, or the tall stems can be cut back completely, before the seeds are scattered. If they are not, prepare for some serious weeding next spring, as fennel seedlings can erupt like cress, taking over everything as soon as your back is turned.

The point of growing herbs in their own area is twofold. From a culinary point of view, having them near to hand to pick as required is easier, when they are gathered in one area, preferably near the kitchen door. More importantly, most of the popular shrubby herbs enjoy similar conditions of uninterrupted sunshine and freely draining soil.

Where the ground is heavy and easily waterlogged, these classic herbs will need to be elevated in a raised bed, of at least twelve inches (30 cm) high, which can be filled with a light, freely draining mix. There are some herbs that require different conditions, however. Parsley does not like to frazzle and is best grown in partial shade in a moisture-retentive, fairly rich soil—likewise, for mint, chives, and the statuesque *Angelica archangelica*. And mint is such a rampant spreader, this is one herb to be sure to grow in a container that confines its conquering tendencies.

Salad Leaves

I REGARD THE SOFT HERBS—CHIVES, BASIL, PARSLEY, CORIANDER (cilantro), and rocket (*Eruca sativa*, or arugula)—as part of the lexicon of "salad leaves," since any of them can contribute to the layered flavors in a summer salad bowl. Chives are easily grown from seeds sown into small pots from late winter onward, with just a pinch of seeds in each pot. If you want lots of chives, they also make a pretty path edging, direct sown in a continuous row; they are very attractive to bees when their flowers open. Once you have chives, it is easy just to dig out and divide the mature clumps into several smaller bunches and replant into fertile soil, in pots or straight in the ground.

For salads generally, a dedicated salad bed is a good idea, where you can keep an eye on things and maintain successional sowings for continuous supplies of leaves. My personal preference is for a raised bed or several large containers, since lifting them away from the ground is the first line of protection against problematic pests, especially slugs and snails. Basil loves the sunshine and is incredibly easy to grow outdoors in the warmest months. It is thirsty, however, and best watered late morning to midday, straight to the roots; avoid sloshing water on the leaves.

There is a bewildering choice when it comes to lettuces, the most versatile and popular of leafy salad crops. Bibb, Boston, or butterhead lettuces produce soft leaves and loose hearts and tend to have a mild, sweet taste. Romaine, or cos lettuces, grow tall and upright, with a loose heart, crisp and succulent; iceberg or crisphead lettuces have dense hearts, best sliced through into crunchy chunks that carry vinaigrettes really well. At the other end of the scale are the loose-leaf, or cut-and-come-again lettuces that can be harvested whole, or just with the outer leaves picked off here and there, as they grow over a long period. Lettuces prefer cool temperatures and in the heat of summer they must have light shade; an open, sunny location is good for spring and autumn crops. If you like the peppery taste of rocket, or arugula, grow it in the same way as lettuce; they make good companion plants, enjoying the same cool-temperature conditions.

←← Beauty combined with productivity: Neat rows of lettuces in variety, joined by feathery fennel, lavender, zucchini, and sweet peas on rustic tepees, among other cottage garden flowers.

← A cottage garden corner, with butterhead lettuce 'Gustav's Salad', a popular Dutch heirloom variety, and an old barrel for a water butt.

17 · Fruit and the Homestead Orchard

What fruit can compare with the Apple for its extended season, lasting from August to June, keeping alive for us in winter, in its sun-stained flush and rustic russet, the memory of golden autumnal days?

— EDWARD BUNYARD

AN ORCHARD IS ONE OF THE OLDEST AND MOST ALLURING KINDS OF garden and a vital part of horticulture across millennia. Cottage gardens typically included some fruit trees, notably apples and/or pears, for making cider or perry (a "cider" made from fermented pear juice). Cider had for centuries been considered safer to drink than water, in areas where water was easily contaminated; indeed, the earliest colonial settlers took cider-making to the New World for the same reason, with the planting of apple trees starting in the Massachusetts Bay Colony and rapidly spreading thereafter. Eventually, most homesteads had an apple orchard and the resulting cider was sometimes used as a currency or barter. This was already a long-established practice in England since Saxon times for payment of tithes, rent, or wages.

Apples respond well to all sorts of pruning and training, enabling even the smallest garden to have a varied orchard of fresh summer and autumn fruits. They can be pinned flat to fences and walls; grown as upright columns or pillars; as branching, miniature trees in pots; or even close to the ground, as knee-high, "step-over" trees, attractively lining a path.

Rootstocks that control ultimate tree sizes were developed hundreds of years ago, to enable such manipulations. They were particularly used in France, where fruit training was—and is—developed to an exceptionally skilled level. With choice fruit varieties grafted onto such "Paradise" rootstocks, as they were collectively called, it was possible to grow more compact trees, which also came into fruit production much earlier than would naturally occur.

The early rootstocks had rather romantic names, such as Doucin Reinette and Jaune de Metz, referencing the tree varieties that supplied them. These were codified in the early twentieth century under commercially brisk titles, such as M7 (more widely available in the United States than in Britain), M9, and various

← Apple harvests can vary from year to year, depending on weather conditions at blossom time and during fruit development, but a tree laden with juicy fruits is a glorious sight for rounding off the growing season.

→→ A secure network of canes makes an excellent screen for growing espalier-trained fruit trees, such as apples. By the time the canes perish, the trees will have developed self-supporting branches in the desired pattern.

others in letter/number combinations. When choosing fruit trees, it is always worthwhile to buy from a specialist nursery that can run through the different rootstock attributes and your local climate as well as suitable pairing varieties for cross-pollination, another important factor.

Pears make majestic, characterful trees over time, but you might also occasionally see one pinned to a sunny cottage wall, with its espaliered arms thrust out left and right, creating level tiers of autumnal fruit, neatly ascending toward the roof eaves. The warmth radiating from a south- or west-facing wall gives a little extra protection to their early blossoms as well as helping fruits develop later on. The popular 'Doyenne du Comice' is one that prefers a warm wall, being slightly more tender than some. The eminent pomologist Edward Bunyard (1879–1939) found much to commend it, including the fruit's "buttery flesh which melts upon the palate with the facility of an ice."

Pear varieties are usually grafted onto Quince A rootstocks in Europe, but OHXF (Old Home and Farmingdale crosses) are used in North America, where cold-hardiness and fire blight resistance are considerations. As with apples, the rootstocks control tree size, making it more manageable and promoting earlier fruits. Pear espaliers create attractive garden partitions and can also be bought as ready-made, step-over trees on the very dwarfing Quince C rootstock.

Quinces themselves (*Cydonia oblonga*) are far less popular fruits, although they make flamboyant trees with conspicuous, shell-pink blossoms and apple- or pear-shaped large fruits, covered in a yellow, downy skin. They always need cooking, to fill pies and flans, perhaps, or convert to jams and jelly. A runcible

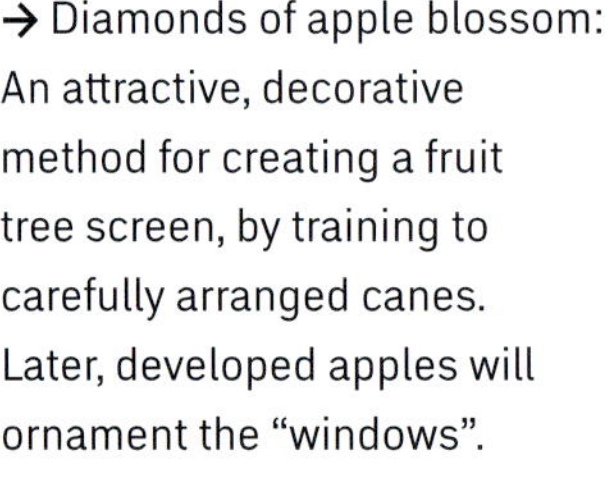
→ Diamonds of apple blossom: An attractive, decorative method for creating a fruit tree screen, by training to carefully arranged canes. Later, developed apples will ornament the "windows".

spoon is not an essential tool for consuming quince, although it was the method preferred by Edward Lear's owl and pussycat. Sometimes, quinces are grown simply to bring indoors, since their October fruits can perfume a room with mingled notes of pear, apple, pineapple, and honey, depending on your olfactory sensitivity. Not very surprisingly, quinces are grown on their own rootstocks and can be trained in similar ways to pear trees. A splayed "fan" shape backed by a sunny fence or wall is a good way of managing one, while getting plenty of fruits from it. As they are self-fertile, there is no practical need for more than one of these interesting trees.

↑ Pear trees enjoy a sunny wall that gives extra protection to their early blossoms. Espalier training suits them well, making the fruit easy to pick when ripe. The 'Munstead' lavender lining the path enhances a cottage garden ambience.

When considering fan-trained trees, plums and apricots should also be mentioned, since this is a superb way to grow both, for generous yields and easy harvesting. For each of these, a great deal of time and effort can be saved by acquiring a young, ready-trained tree for a south-facing wall. As always, one's particular location, climate, and soil type will be factors to consider, along with taste and texture preferences. This is where a local specialist nursery will again be invaluable.

Soft Fruits: Cottage Garden Currants and Berries

Plants of "soft fruits" are shorter in stature and shorter-lived than tree fruits and most of the popular ones fall into two kinds. First, there are those which make bushes—gooseberries and their close relatives, the currants (red-, white, and blackcurrants). These traditional cottage garden plants develop a permanent, shrubby framework and are easy to grow and enjoy a position in dappled shade, rather than full-on sunshine and too much heat. Secondly, there are the cane fruits, more of which in a moment.

In very limited space, or for ornamental reasons, gooseberries and currants can be pruned and shaped into standards (i.e., "lollipops" on a clear stem), or against a wall as fans, rather like the tree fruits. Once established, these decorative methods make routine pruning and harvesting easy. Gooseberries, redcurrants, and white currants are often grown as single cordons, a method not suited to blackcurrants; however, blackcurrants can make nice little half-standard "trees" when grafted onto a rootstock stem of the closely related *Ribes aureum*. Specialist nurseries sometimes sell them in this way, but they are painstaking and time consuming to shape and develop and are therefore correspondingly

↑ Along with many other soft fruits, raspberries benefit from the protection a fruit cage gives them from various garden wildlife.

← Hanging in generous bunches, juicy red currants are easy to harvest when grown as half-standard trees. Permanent staking with a sturdy pole is required so the plant does not topple over when in fruit.

more expensive than a typical bush. Although this kind of training makes harvesting the berries easy, the "head" becomes top-heavy when in fruit and permanent support of the plant with a suitable stake is required.

Cane fruits, on the other hand, produce new stems or canes from the ground every year. Raspberries, blackberries, and hybrid berries of various kinds fall into this category. They are best trained against a system of parallel wires or a wooden trellis, to keep their potentially unruly canes in order. For prolonging the raspberry season, the autumn-fruiting varieties, such as 'Autumn Bliss' and 'Fallgold', produce small crops of sweet berries and are very easy to grow. As they fruit on new wood, you can cut down all the canes after the harvest. Being less vigorous than summer raspberries, they make good container-grown plants too.

All of the above fruits can be worked into the cottage-inspired garden setting in numerous attractive ways among ornamental plants; but their soft leaves and buds, and the tempting juiciness of the fruits in due season, make currants and berries incredibly vulnerable to a variety of wildlife, including slugs, sawflies, and especially birds. For this reason, the best way to grow currants and berries for a meaningful home harvest is within the protection of a fruit cage, which at least fends off the birds and, depending on mesh size, perhaps one or two other pests. (Bear in mind, though, at flowering time, you do want the netting to be open enough to give access to pollinating insects; standard fruit cage netting allows for this.) Depending on the available space, the fruit cage can be a large-framed, walk-in structure with a full-height door, or something much more modest: just enough to cover a couple of bushes, or a short row of canes.

As low-growing herbaceous perennials, strawberries can be grown anywhere that is sufficiently warm and sunny. (Where there is space, they will benefit from a fruit cage's bird protection.) Strawberries are sufficiently versatile to be grown in various decorative ways: edging a path or a border, for example, or in a raised bed. Having attractive leaves and flowers as well as delicious fruits, strawberries are excellent for patio containers. Alpine, or wild strawberries (*Fragaria vesca*)

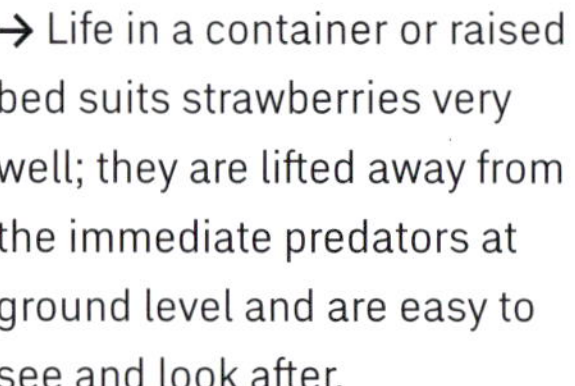

→ Life in a container or raised bed suits strawberries very well; they are lifted away from the immediate predators at ground level and are easy to see and look after.

↑ Soft fruits for various circumstances, left to right: [left] Tayberries, a blackberry-raspberry hybrid, enjoy the support of a sturdy trellis. [center] Gooseberries 'Invicta' and 'Whinham's Industry' can make attractive standard trees or topiaries. [right] When grown in pots, blueberry bushes can be given precisely the sort of acidic soil they require.

have very small fruits with a distinctive flavor. They are very decorative in pots, where their fruits dangle in small bunches over the edges. They also make pretty path edgings and crop continuously from early to late summer.

Hybrid "everbearing" or perpetual strawberries are an interesting development, producing an early crop and then a later one. Among them, 'Mara des Bois' has long been popular with chefs. The highly regarded 'Toscana', 'Berries Galore Rose', and 'Tarpan' are among those that have unusual, dark pink flowers before they fruit.

Robins, blackbirds, finches, and thrushes all very much enjoy eating strawberries (think of William Morris's famous fabric design, "Strawberry Thief," featuring a well-fed thrush). Planting a row of alpine strawberries along the path edge is a nice gift for foraging garden birds (and they will also eat the slugs that are sure to be lurking nearby!).

Requiring a strongly acidic soil of pH 4–5.5, blueberries can only be grown by many of us when planted in a raised bed or a container, which can be filled with a proprietary ericaceous potting mix. As part of the heather family *Ericaceae*, they share with heathers clusters of attractive, flagon-shaped flowers, beloved by bees. Feeding with fertilizer tailored to acid-loving plants and regular watering with rainwater will encourage the plant's health and development of the delicious berries in due course.

As with fruit trees, it is best to buy soft fruits from a specialist nursery that will not only have the largest range to choose from, but can be helpful regarding any specific disease resistance or climate requirements appropriate to your location.

18 · Sustainable Strategies

A FRIEND SAID TO ME RECENTLY, "I'M JUST NO GOOD AT GARDENING. The plants I buy always die; I just haven't got green fingers. . . ." For anyone new to gardening, or those who have struggled to succeed in growing anything so far, there is hope—lots of it. The secret is this: You only need to know and act upon two things to start seeing success. First, determine what sort of soil you are dealing with. Second, know which areas of your outdoor space get plenty of sunshine and which do not. Just finding out these two fundamentals—and adjusting your plant choices accordingly—can help recapture your confidence.

A basic pH soil test kit, very easily purchased from garden stores and online, gives helpful guidance as to whether one's garden soil is acidic, neutral, or alkaline. It does this by measuring the concentration of hydrogen ions in solution: the greater the concentration of ions, the more acidic the soil. The soil's pH affects how well plants can absorb essential nutrients, and the test will be a guide to your ground's potential strengths or weaknesses, in relation to particular plants' requirements.

We have all done this in basic school chemistry, comparing the acidity or alkalinity of a solution against a colored scale numbered from 0 to 14: The figure 7 in the middle indicates neutral pH, where the concentration of hydrogen and hydroxide ions balance each other out. A lower than 7 pH reading leans toward acidity—the lower the number indicated, the more acidic the soil. Conversely, a higher reading, above 7, indicates that the soil is more alkaline. Certain plants, such as camellias, rhododendrons, azaleas, and heathers, prefer to be on the acidic side of neutral, around 5 to 6; blueberries, huckleberries, and their kind like it even more acidic, around 4.5 to 5.5. Nevertheless, many more plants enjoy neutral ground, close to 7, or very slightly higher. Lilacs, lavenders, thymes, clematis, boxwoods, and yews are examples; also, cabbages and their ilk. Just a casual walk around the community, noticing the plants that are thriving, can give a preliminary indication of which plants are likely to grow with ease.

Soil texture and structure are important too, since they dictate how well the roots of plants will thrive and take up water and nutrients. Added organic

← Traditional rainwater collection, among cottage garden staples, including pansies, thyme, columbines, foxgloves, and sorrel. Stinging nettles *Urtica dioica* are an important food source for the caterpillars of several butterfly species.

→→ After more than a century and a half, apex-roofed, Victorian-style greenhouses are still the most popular design, being practical, attractive, and versatile (p. 264).

↑ Caring for the strawberry crop: A mulch of straw has several benefits, maintaining even soil temperature, retaining soil moisture, and lifting the berries off the ground, keeping them clean and unlikely to rot. Well-fixed netting prevents bird predation.

materials, such as well-rotted animal manures and garden composts universally help improve soil fertility. They open up heavy, clay ground, improving the structure and getting the earthworms working to increase aeration. They are also invaluable when added to light, sandy, stony, or chalky soils, giving them more substance and helping trap moisture and nutrients that would otherwise rapidly drain away.

Composts and manures help build the soil biome, increasing the communities of microorganisms that play a vital role in soil and plant health. Once you are active in the garden, creating a composting area becomes second nature—a place where prunings, mowings, leaf sweepings, and other vegetable remains can be piled together to rot into dark crumbs. In this respect, a domestic garden shredder capable of chopping or crushing woody prunings from roses, fruit trees, and shrubs is helpful, speeding up the composting rate.

Once rotted, your homemade compost can be returned to the soil to enrich it. Even in small gardens, discreet, ready-made bins do this really well, and some are quite attractively disguised, such as the wooden "traditional beehive" design, with a hinge-opening lid. There is far more to know about the topic of soil microbiomes than space allows within these pages, of course, but plenty of online resources go into greater detail, if you require further help.

Another reason why people sometimes think they are failures at gardening has to do with commercial potting composts. Many of them these days—at least in Britain—consist of bagged composted material sourced from the waste recycling departments of local authorities. While it is good that they do such a service, the quality of the end products, branded and bagged as "multipurpose" potting mix, can frequently be poor. I have found all sorts of things in them, including sticks, stones, pieces of wire, scraps of fabric, even shards of glass, and shreds of plastics. The composts themselves are compacted, dense, and airless in their shrink-wrapped packaging, so it is not surprising that some plants may struggle to thrive when plunged into this stuff.

What is the answer? Professional-grade composts from specialty suppliers are considerably better but tend to be more expensive. For containers, professional mixes are worth using to fill the top one-third or half, where a young plant's roots need to become established. I usually find that, wherever the potting mix is from, some further aeration is needed with an added dose of perlite or vermiculite, or both (they are pH neutral), well mixed in. It is incredible how much improvement is to be had from just doing this, so that roots can breathe and grow. Bagged ericaceous composts are very useful for filling raised beds and pots that will be home to lime-hating plants.

↓ Homemade compost is a great soil enricher. Since squashes are very heavy feeders, they enjoy growing on the maturing compost, in this case assisted by a trellis.

Location, Location, Location

I mentioned at the start that the second crucial bit of knowledge a gardener needs is an understanding of where there is plenty of sunshine in the garden, where there is permanent shade, and where there is a bit of both—sunshine just in the morning, for example, or where the shadow of trees or buildings changes light conditions for part of the day as the sun moves around. The familiar real estate agent's mantra of "location, location, location" definitely applies to plants.

Most Mediterranean herbs, for example, such as lavender, thyme, oregano, phlomis, sage, santolina, and various silver-leaved species, love to bask in full sunshine. Likewise, tomatoes, peppers, and many more fruits and vegetables—although not all. On the other hand, various mints, parsley, Angelica, ferns, Japanese anemones, hydrangeas, heucheras, and foxgloves are among the shade lovers. Choosing plants according to their preferred location can forestall a lot of potential woes.

↓ Water-conscious gravel gardening for a Mediterranean-type environment: Harmoniously blending clouds of *Stachys cretica*, *Euphorbia rigida*, *Achillea crithmifolia*, *Salvia amplexicaule*, *Teucrium hircanicum*, and *Salvia sclarea* var. *turkestanica*.

Conserving Water

Those of us who live in the far southeast of England are used to prolonged dry periods every few years along with watering bans. It always seems strange to me that various societies in the ancient world were able to transport water across hundreds of miles, via carefully calibrated aqueducts and tunnels, but nobody in our diminutive island has ever had the wit to engineer the transportation of excess water from the rainy northern and western regions to the drier, and very highly populated, southeast. So, we collect rainwater, diverted from gutters and downpipes into butts and barrels, and choose our plants carefully.

↖ A stony mulch helps conserve soil moisture and prevent the establishment of weeds among the lavender.

↑ One of the so-called Jerusalem sages, *Phlomis purpurea*, is a pretty shrub for low water and Mediterranean climate gardens, and native to Spain and Portugal.

Carefully collecting rain is nothing new, of course. Gertrude Jekyll's own photographs of village cottage gardens show that roof rainwater was channeled into sturdy barrels, placed alongside homes that predated piped running water. Similar rainwater barrels can be seen in photographs of Lutyens's early country houses. The "tanks" (formal ponds) that feature in so many gardens made by Lutyens and Jekyll were dual purpose, being ornamental but also serviceable "dipping ponds," where watering cans could be filled to irrigate nearby plants.

Resilient Planting Pioneers

When we speak today of making our gardens more weather resilient, how we do it will depend on local conditions. Gravel gardens have received a lot of converts since Joyce Robinson (1904–1996), a market gardener and farmer, made what is probably Britain's first, in 1970. Following a transformative holiday in 1969

←← Joyce Robinson's experimental gravel garden, begun in 1970. Its stony beds include silvery lamb's ears *Stachys byzantina*, red-hot pokers *Kniphofia nobilis*, *Astelia chathamica*, heleniums, and *Aster* x *frikartiii* 'Monch'.

walking in the herb-rich, stony landscapes of the Greek Islands, on returning home, she almost immediately removed the vegetables in the walled garden at Denmans, her home near the Sussex coast. The kitchen garden staples were replaced by an informal cottage garden of herbs, tough shrubs, and self-sown flowers, carefully edited to maintain a balance. The area was heavily mulched with water-worn gravel, a local material still harvested from the nearby seashore.

Delighted with the effect, Robinson developed another area with gravel in 1972 and, in 1977, her pièce de résistance, on a former cow paddock, where the free-draining ground slopes gently southward. Here, she made sweeping, serpentine swaths of water-worn gravel and pebbles, imitating a meandering river.

"Larger, rounded sea-bed stones were thrown up unevenly against the bank and we planted only things that might be found growing in a dry stream bed: grasses, iris, thistles, mint, willow, and elder," she noted in her memoir, *Glorious Disarray* (1989). Striking architectural plants, such as the silvery, paddle-leaved mullein, *Verbascum bombyciferum*, euphorbias, the downy, silver sage *Salvia argentea*, and milk thistle *Silybum marianum*, were allowed to self-sow "in sympathy with the whole natural scene."

From 1980, the garden at Denmans came to be managed by John Brookes (1933–2018), the internationally renowned landscape designer, who immensely admired Robinson's originality, recalling:

> Joyce had managed to group and contrast her planting in an extraordinary way. On the one hand totally out of control in its exuberance, but on the other hand structured to contain the exuberance. . . . [It] was at the time unique, for it seemed to pioneer a type of decorative gardening from which we have all learned since.

In the 1980s, I visited Denmans many times, sometimes encountering Robinson zooming about the garden in her mobility scooter, always happy to pause and chat. John Brookes continued to cherish and develop the garden at Denmans until his death, making it his home, design studio, and teaching base.

A different kind of resilient gravel garden was created by John Bond (1932–2001), head of the royal gardens at Windsor. In 1990, he showed me around the experimental Dry Garden he had made in 1977, in a small part of the exemplary Savill Garden at Windsor. Planted in direct response to an extended drought and an unusually hot summer in 1976, its gravel beds contained resilient species, such as the hybrid strawberry tree of Greece, *Arbutus* × *andrachnoides*, prairie grasses, South African red-hot pokers (*Kniphofia* spp.), euphorbias in variety, and Mediterranean bulbs.

The most extreme example of gravel gardening—and one of the most influential—was made in the mid-1980s by the filmmaker Derek Jarman (1942–1994), at his former fisherman's cottage, right on the shingle (pebble) beach at Dungeness, Kent. It was (and is) a work of art and ecological planting, combining the characterful stones of the beach and found pieces of driftwood,

↑ Attractive partners for a mild-climate, graveled area: The Mexican feather grass *Stipa tenuissima* highlights lavenders and pretty pink *Tulbaghia violacea*.

with the flowers of the seashore, that withstand wind and salt spray. Many seaside cottage gardens have been inspired by it—and plenty of inland cottages too, where the owners have wanted to create an escape with coastal ambience.

Gardening in Essex, one of the drier eastern counties in England, Beth Chatto packed much good advice into her first book, *The Dry Garden* (1978), particularly regarding "Dry Sun," versus "Dry Shade," and the plants for each. She highlighted the importance of incorporating garden compost for soil conditioning prior to planting, whatever sort of ground you are dealing with. By the time *Beth Chatto's Gravel Garden* was published in 2000, the advantages of choosing the right plant for the right place (as trialed in the new gravel garden she had made from 1992 onward), was exciting and alluring. Relaxed and somewhat Mediterranean in plant choice, it might be considered a sophisticated country-cottage-style garden for a more resilient and water-conscious age.

All of the above-mentioned gardens still exist and are very regularly opened to visitors to study and make useful notes. One could say that they have proved another sort of resilience, in their longevity and continued influence.

Protecting What You Are Growing

→ People have come up with numerous ingenious methods for protecting plants from external forces, be they weather or wildlife.

CLOCKWISE, FROM TOP LEFT:
— Bamboo cloches pinned to the ground keep birds at bay
— Net bags protect maturing grapes from birds and rodents
— A "racing driver" scarecrow looks as if it means business
— Heavy, wind-resistant glass cloches protect vulnerable crops

Typical cottage garden flowers are, by nature, hardy, with little or no requirement for mollycoddling. Nevertheless, the keen gardener, sooner or later, may not be able to resist the allure of a greenhouse of whatever size suits both space and purse. It has numerous uses, depending on one's interests—perhaps for overwintering salads, raising successional microgreens, maintaining nonhardy potted plants, starting off early seeds, or taking cuttings of special plants.

In many areas, tomatoes, peppers, and cucumbers have a far better chance of cropping in a greenhouse than outdoors. Under glass, they can be started early in the season and grow happily, sheltered from cold winds, while receiving maximum light. The caveat, of course, is that the greenhouse is somewhere that must be visited frequently, for checking plant welfare, watering as needed, adjusting ventilation, and even providing extra warmth or light, if necessary. In such a closed environment, targeted biological pest controls are effective, coupled with companion planting of aromatic species, such as tagetes and basils. And perhaps one should not underestimate the simple pleasure of just pottering, in a sheltered and congenial place among the plants, when the wind is raging, or the rain pit-patting down on the windowpanes.

Whereas the greenhouse is a confined and controlled environment, and therefore easy to manage, outdoors one is always trying to achieve a balance between enjoyment of local wildlife and prevention of destructive overbrowsing. There is no way of stopping foraging deer, foxes, or rabbits, unless adequate fencing of appropriate design and height is erected, preferably by a professional, to keep them out. Certain ornamental berrying plants I am happy for the birds to eat (chiefly, the berries that we do *not* want to eat). For the rest, raspberries, gooseberries, and the various currants are safest from birds in the protection of a fruit cage. Cloches are great for protecting individual plants during their vulnerable moments. The bamboo type, when securely anchored around the base, gives adequate temporary protection against pigeons and pheasants and a measure of shade, if required. Heavy glass cloches are not only good for weather shelter, but also for protection against birds, rodents, slugs, and snails.

Perhaps the most fun of all (though, unfortunately, not necessarily the most effective) is the scarecrow. A device used since ancient times in one form or another, the model of a dressed, human figure (often it is stuffed with straw), may have temporary effect, especially if wind-mobile items such as ribbons, or reflective CDs (remember those?), are attached. The ingeniousness of gardeners in dressing their homemade scarecrows is a delightful folk art and very much part of the cottage garden vernacular.

Acknowledgments

My huge thanks to Charles Miers at Rizzoli for inviting me to write *Cottage Gardens*. This is the third book I have had the pleasure of preparing for Rizzoli, and I am always impressed by their great professionalism and attention to detail. I am most grateful to Klaus Kirschbaum for his kind and considerate steering and editing and to the team whose combined talents have created such a beautiful and engaging product. Robert Dalrymple has designed *Cottage Gardens* with his customary flair and sympathy for the topics covered, so that I feel uplifted and inspired when I look through these pages.

I have had the pleasure of working with Marianne Majerus for very many years, and her photography is second to none. From cover to cover, Marianne's beautiful photographs of these cottages and their gardens and plants capture the delights of every season. Such engaging places do not make themselves, of course, and my thanks are also warmly sent to the makers of these inspiring gardens.

—KATHRYN BRADLEY-HOLE

My thanks go to: Kathryn Bradley-Hole for her inspiring words and her friendship and collaboration over many years.

The editors at Rizzoli International Publications for involving me in making this beautiful book. Klaus Kirschbaum and Robert Dalrymple for their vision and patience in bringing this project to fruition.

The many garden friends and designers for the pleasure and privilege of photographing their gardens.

—MARIANNE MAJERUS

Further Reading

Aslet, Clive. *The Arts & Crafts Country House*. Aurum Press, 2011

Austin, David. *The Rose*. Garden Art Press/Antique Collectors Club, 2009

Bisgrove, Richard. *William Robinson: The Wild Gardener*. Frances Lincoln, 2008

Blanc, Raymond. *Kew on a Plate With Raymond Blanc: Recipes, Horticulture and Heritage*. Headline, 2015

Bloom, Adrian. *Winter Garden Glory*. HarperCollins, 1993

Bloom, Alan. *Alan Bloom's Hardy Perennials*. Batsford, 1991

Bradley-Hole, Kathryn. *English Gardens from the Archives of* Country Life *Magazine*. Rizzoli, 2019

Bradley-Hole, Kathryn. *The Naturally Beautiful Garden: Designs that Engage with Wildlife and Nature*. Rizzoli, 2021

Brookes, John. *The Country Garden*. DK, 1987

Brookes, John. *Planting the Country Way: A Hands-on Approach*. BBC, 1994

Brown, Jane. *Gardens of a Golden Afternoon: The Story of a Partnership: Edwin Lutyens and Gertrude Jekyll*. Allen Lane, 1982

Brown, Jane. *Vita's Other World: A Gardening Biography of Vita Sackville-West*. Penguin, 1987

Buchan, Ursula. *Garden People: Valerie Finnis and the Golden Age of Gardening*. Thames & Hudson, 2007

Bunyard, Edward A. *The Anatomy of Dessert*. Random House/Modern Library, 2006

Bunyard, Edward & Lorna. *The Epicure's Companion*. J. M. Dent, 1937

Bunyard, Edward A. *Old Garden Roses*. Country Life, 1936

Campbell, Susan. *Charleston Kedding, A History of Kitchen Gardening*. Ebury Press, 1996

Chatto, Beth. *Beth Chatto's Gravel Garden*. Frances Lincoln, 2000

Chatto, Beth. *The Damp Garden*. J. M. Dent, 1993

Chatto, Beth. *The Dry Garden*. J. M. Dent, 1993

Cottage Garden Society, The. *The Cottage Gardener's Companion*. David & Charles, 1993

Dalby, Claus. *The Cottage Garden*. Quarto, 2023

Darke, Rick. *Timber Pocket Guide to Ornamental Grasses*. Timber Press, 2004

Davies, Jennifer. *The Victorian Flower Garden*. BBC, 1991

Davies, Jennifer. *The Victorian Kitchen Garden*. BBC, 1987

de Thame, Rachel. *A Flower Garden for Pollinators*. Greenfinch, 2024

Diacono, Mark. *A Year at Otter Farm*. Bloomsbury, 2014

Diacono, Mark. *The River Cottage Veg Patch Handbook*. Bloomsbury, 2009

Don, Monty. *Down to Earth: Gardening Wisdom*. DK, 2017

Dowding, Charles. *Compost: Transform Waste into New Life*. DK, 2024

Dowding, Charles. *No Dig: Nurture Your Soil to Grow Better Veg with Less Effort*. DK, 2022

Duthie, Ruth. *Florists' Flowers and Societies*. Shire Press, 1988

Elgood, George S., and Gertrude Jeckyll. *Some English Gardens*. Longmans, Green & Co., 1905

Elliott, Brent. *Victorian Gardens*. Batsford, 1986

Festing, Sally. *Gertrude Jekyll*. Viking, 1991

Filippi, Olivier. *The Dry Gardening Handbook*. Filbert Press, 2019

Fish, Margery. *A Flower for Every Day*. Studio Vista, 1965

Fish, Margery. *We Made a Garden*. Collingridge, 1956

Flowerdew, Bob. *Bob Flowerdew's Complete Fruit Book*. Kyle Cathie, 1995

Frost, Adam. *RHS How to Create Your Garden*. DK, 2019

Guillet, Dominique. *The Seeds of Kokopelli: A Manual for the Production of Seeds in the Family Garden*. Kokopelli Seed Foundation, 2002

Hall, Tony. *Gardening With Drought Friendly Plants*. Kew Publishing, 2020

Halliwell, Brian. *Old Garden Flowers*. Bishopsgate Press, 1987

Hamilton, Geoff. *Organic Gardening*. DK, 1987

Hamilton, Geoff. *The Ornamental Kitchen Garden*. BBC, 1990

Hamilton, Jill, Duchess of, Penny Hart, and John Simmons. *The Gardens of William Morris*. Frances Lincoln, 1998

Hatch, Peter J. *The Fruits and Fruit Trees of Monticello*. University Press of Virginia, 1998

Ikin, Caroline. *The Victorian Garden*. Shire Press, 2012

Jarman, Derek. *Derek Jarman's Garden*. Thames & Hudson, 1995

Jekyll, Gertrude. *Colour in the Flower Garden*. Country Life, 1908

Jekyll, Gertrude. *Home and Garden*. Longmans, Green & Co., 1900

Jekyll, Gertrude. *Old West Surrey*. Longmans, Green & Co., 1904

Johnson, Hugh. *The Principles of Gardening*. Mitchell Beazley, 1979

Kingsbury, Noel. *Natural Garden Style: Gardening Inspired by Nature*. Merrell, 2009

Lacey, Stephen. *Gardens of the National Trust*. National Trust, 1996

Lacey, Stephen. *Scent in Your Garden*. Frances Lincoln, 1991

Lane, Clive. *Cottage Garden Annuals*. David & Charles, 1997

Larkcom, Joy. *Oriental Vegetables*. John Murray, 1991

Lawson, Andrew. *The Gardener's Book of Colour*. Frances Lincoln, 1996

Lloyd, Christopher. *The Well-Tempered Garden*. Collins, 1970

Lloyd, Christopher. *The Year at Great Dixter*. Viking, 1987

Loades, Greg. *The Modern Cottage Garden: A Fresh Approach to a Classic Style*. Timber Press, 2020

Marshall, Beth. *Grow Yourself Healthy*. Frances Lincoln, 2020

Mason, Anna. *William Morris*. Thames & Hudson/V&A, 2021

Massingham, Betty. *Miss Jekyll, Portrait of a Great Gardener*. Country Life, 1966

McIntyre, Anne. *The Good Health Garden: Growing and Using Healing Foods*. Reader's Digest, 1998

McMorland Hunter, Jane, and Chris Kelly. *For the Love of an Orchard*. Pavilion, 2010

McVicar, Jekka. *Jekka's Complete Herb Book*. Kyle Cathie, 1994

McTernan, Cinead. *Kitchen Garden Experts*. Frances Lincoln, 2014

Nichols, Beverley. *Merry Hall* (facsimile edition). Timber Press, 1998

Osler, Mirabel. *A Gentle Plea for Chaos*. Bloomsbury, 1989

Ottewill, David. *The Edwardian Garden*. Yale University Press, 1989

Oudolf, Piet, and Henk Gerritsen. *Planting the Natural Garden*. Timber Press, 2019

Page, Russell. *The Education of a Gardener*. Harvill, 1994

Parkinson, Arthur. *The Pottery Gardener*. The History Press, 2018

Phillips, Roger, and Martin Rix. *Vegetables*. Pan, 2021

Pope, Nori and Sandra. *Colour by Design*. Conran Octopus, 1998

Powell, Christopher. *Discovering Cottage Architecture*. Shire Press, 1984

Raven, Sarah. *The Great Vegetable Plot*. BBC, 2005

Richardson, Tim. *English Gardens in the Twentieth Century*. Aurum Press, 2005

Robinson, William. *The English Flower Garden and Home Grounds*. 9th ed. John Murray, 1905

Robinson, William. *Home Landscapes*. John Murray, 1914

Robinson, William. *The English Flower Garden and Home Grounds*, 9th ed. John Murray, 1905

Robinson, William. *The Wild Garden*. 5th ed. John Murray, 1903

Rohde, Eleanour Sinclair. *The Story of the Garden*. Medici Society, 1932

RHS. *The RHS Complete Gardener's Manual*. DK, 2020

RHS. *Your Wellbeing Garden*. DK, 2020

Rutherford, Sarah. *The Arts and Crafts Garden*. Shire Press, 2013

Sackville-West, V. *Country Notes*. Michael Joseph, 1939

Sackville-West, V. *The Illustrated Garden Book. A New Anthology by Robin Lane Fox*. Michael Joseph, 1986

Sanecki, Kay. *History of the English Herb Garden*. Ward Lock, 1992

Sankey, Andrew. *The English Cottage Garden*. The Crowood Press, 2021

Scarman, John. *Gardening With Old Roses*. HarperCollins, 1996

Scott-James, Anne. *Sissinghurst: The Making of a Garden*. Michael Joseph, 1975

Segall, Barbara. *The Herb Garden, Month-by-Month*. David & Charles, 1994

Simms, Barbara. *John Brookes: Garden and Landscape Designer*. Conran Octopus, 2007

Tankard, Judith B. *Gertrude Jekyll and the Country House Garden*. Aurum Press, 2011

Tankard, Judith B., and Martin A. Wood. *Gertrude Jekyll at Munstead Wood*. Sutton, 1996

Thomas, Graham Stuart. *Perennial Garden Plants: The Modern Florilegium*. 3rd ed. J. M. Dent, 1993

Thompson, Peter. *The Self-Sustaining Garden: The Guide to Matrix Planting*. Frances Lincoln, 2007

Titchmarsh, Alan. *How to Garden: Perennial Garden Plants*. BBC, 2010

Titchmarsh, Alan. *How to Garden: Small Gardens*. BBC, 2016

Verey, Rosemary. *Rosemary Verey's Making of a Garden*. Frances Lincoln, 1995

Verey, Rosemary. *The Scented Garden*. Michael Joseph, 1995

Way, Twigs. *The Cottage Garden*. Shire Press, 2011

Weaver, Sir Lawrence. *Cottages*. Country Life, 1926

Weaver, Sir Lawrence. *Houses and Gardens by Sir Edwin Lutyens, R.A.* Life, 1925

Weaver, William Woys. *Heirloom Vegetable Gardening: A Master Gardener's Guide to Planting, Seed Saving, and Cultural History*. Quarto, 2018

Whitsey, Fred. *The Garden at Hidcote*. Frances Lincoln, 2007

Woodforde, John. *The Truth About Cottages*. Routledge, Kegan & Paul, 1969

WEBSITES

Colonial Williamsburg
www.colonialwilliamsburg.org

Cottage Garden Society
www.thecgs.org.uk

Country Life
www.countrylife.co.uk

Garden Museum
www.gardenmuseum.org.uk

Gardens Trust
www.thegardenstrust.org

Gertrude Jekyll official website
www.gertrudejekyll.co.uk

Gravetye Manor
www.gravetyemanor.co.uk

Hardy Plant Society
www.hardy-plant.org.uk

National Garden Scheme
www.ngs.org.uk

National Trust
www.nationaltrust.org.uk

Royal Horticultural Society
www.rhs.org.uk

Victoria and Albert Museum
www.vam.ac.uk

William Morris Gallery
www.wmgallery.org.uk

Image Credits

All of the photographs in this book were taken by Marianne Majerus.

LOCATIONS & DESIGNERS

Arundel Castle, West Sussex, England: 64, 159

Ballymaloe Cookery School, Ireland: 226

Barnsley House, Gloucestershire, England: 39, 53

Clergy House, Alfriston, England: 20, 30

Colonial Williamsburg, Virginia, USA: 1, 40, 42, 44

Coughton Court, Warwickshire, England: 246

Denmans, Sussex, England: 260

Design: Acres Wild: 90, 126, 189, 197, 204

Design: Arabella Lennox-Boyd: 247

Design: Beth Marshall: 210

Design: Christopher Bradley-Hole: 178

Design: Tommaso del Buono and Paul Gazerwitz: 240

Design: Dominick Murphy: 176, 188

Design: Emma Griffin: 244

Design: Françoise Maas: 76, 203

Design: Gaston Kemp: 39

Design: Gilbert Folschette: 82

Design: Graham Lloyd-Brunt: 164

Design: Ian Kitson: 50, 53

Design: James and Anne Halliday: 174

Design: James and Helen Basson, Scape Design: 258

Design: Jane Brockbank: 53

Design: Jilayne Rickards: 80

Design: Juan Carlos Cure: 161

Design: Julie Toll: 36, 146, 224

Design: Kate Stuart Smith: 74, 238

Design: Lucy Sommers: 184

Design: Marian Boswall: 137

Design: Marianne Jacoby: 234

Design: Marianne Majerus: 16, 108

Design: Marie-France Koos: 112, 198

Design: Mariette Schank: 14

Design: Mark Gregory: 252

Design: Mary Keen: 46

Design: Mireille Ferrari: 38

Design: Murphy & Sheanon: 53

Design: Nigel Watts: 161

Design: Paul Hammes: 144, 192

Design: Robin and Rosie Lloyd: 26

Design: Sarah Cook: 10

Design: Sean Walter: 53, 154, 200

Design: Sir Terence Conran: 196

Design: Stuart Craine: 48

Design: Sue Townsend: 53, 182

Design: Tom Stuart-Smith: 78, 98, 186, 190, 263

Design: Tom Stuart-Smith and James Hitchmough: 177

Design: Tony Woods, Garden Club London: 75

Design: Val Bourne: 161

Design: Woodhouse Natural Pools: 191

Dove Cottage, Yorkshire, England: 158

East Lambrook Manor, Somerset, England: 66, 68, 69

Furzelea, Essex, England: 37

Grafton Cottage, Staffordshire, England: 103, 100, 122

Gravetye Manor, West Sussex, England: 142

Great Dixter, East Sussex, England: 58

Haddon Hall, Derbyshire, England: 34

Haddon Lake House, Isle of Wight, England: 134

Haseley Court, Oxfordshire, England: 39

Hestercombe House and Gardens, Somerset, England: 140, 143

Jordans Mill, Bedfordhire, England: 202

Knowle Hill Farm, Kent, England: 4

Lady Bird Johnson Wildflower Center, Austin, Texas, USA: Endpapers

Le Domaine viticole Claude Bentz, Luxembourg: 148, 257

Le Jardin de Berchigranges, France: 53

Le Jardin Secret, Marrakesh, Morocco (Design: Tom Stuart-Smith): 263

Long House Plants, Essex, England: 104, 136

Manor House Farm, Norfolk, England: 6

Old Bladbean Stud, Kent, England: 71, 254

Parc Thermal de Mondorf-les-Bains, Luxembourg: 116

Petersfield Physic Garden, Hampshire, England: 39

RHS Garden, Hyde Hall, Essex, England: 227

Sissinghurst Castle, Kent, England: 118, 120

Kathy Brown's Garden, The Manor House, Stevington, Bedfordshire, England: 70, 92, 152

The Manor, Hemingford Grey, Cambridgeshire, England: 18, 84

Theobald's Farmhouse, London, England: 32

Tinkers Green Farm, Essex, England: 72, 265

Ulting Wick, Essex, England: 132, 222

Yews Farm, Somerset, England: 156

York Gate Garden, West Yorkshire, England: 54

ADDITIONAL SOURCES

Page 8: Courtesy of National Gallery of Art, Washington, DC

Page 22: Photo from *The Arts & Crafts Country House*, by Clive Aslet (Aurum Press, 2011)

Page 23: Photo from *The Lost Gardens of England*, by Kathryn Bradley-Hole (Aurum Press, 2004)

Pages 24 and 28: Art from *Some English Gardens*, by George S. Elgood and Gertrude Jekyll (Longmans, Green & Co., 1905)

Index

First published in English in the United States of America in 2026 by

Rizzoli International Publications, Inc.
49 West 27th Street · New York, NY 10001
www.rizzoliusa.com

Publisher: Charles Miers
Editor: Klaus Kirschbaum
Assistant Editor: Emily Ligniti
Design: Robert Dalrymple
Production Manager: Maria Pia Gramaglia
Managing Editor: Lynn Scrabis

ISBN-13: 978-0-8478-7615-0
Library of Congress Catalog Control Number: 2025943260

Printed in Singapore
2026 2027 2028 2029 / 10 9 8 7 6 5 4 3 2 1

The authorized representative in the EU for product safety and compliance is
Mondadori Libri S.p.A., via Gian Battista Vico 42, 20123 Milan, Italy
www.mondadori.it

Front jacket: Rosa 'Raubritter' on blue painted arch. Poppy Cottage, Cornwall.

Binding design: *Pathways* by Alice Pattullo from Hamilton Weston Wallpapers Ltd.

Endpapers: The coral honeysuckle, *Lonicera sempervirens*, ornaments a picket fence.

Page 1: Glass cloches at Colonial Williamsburg, Virginia.

Pages 2–3: Annual poppies, *Papaver somniferum*.

Page 4: Plenty of seats invite relaxation in a classic cottage garden, with summer flowers including pink roses 'Gertrude Jekyll' and 'Old Blush China' beyond a froth of white Orlaya grandiflora.

Pages 6–7: Vigorous and wide spreading, the popular old rambler rose, 'Rambling Rector' blossoms at midsummer in an avalanche of creamy-white, fragrant flowers, much enjoyed by bees.

Back jacket: Kitchen garden with rows of fennel, lettuce, lavender, and sweet peas on bamboo cane wigwams.

Visit us online:
Facebook.com/RizzoliNewYork
Instagram.com/RizzoliBooks
Youtube.com/user/RizzoliNY